THE CHALLENGES OF CHANGE

THE CHALLENGES OF CHANGE

Walter Cronkite

FOREWORD BY IRVING DILLIARD

Public Affairs Press, Washington, D. C.

419 New Jersey Ave., Washington, D.C. 20003
Printed in the United States of America
Library of Congress Catalog Card No. 71-149494

FOREWORD

It would seem presumptuous of almost anyone to write an introduction of any kind for Walter Cronkite or, as in this instance, for a collection of his leading public addresses.

In all our two hundred million plus population, his is one of the most readily recognized faces, his one of the most easily identified voices. He comes daily into literally countless homes with news of the world for the rest of us. He is a familiar, welcome visitor, reassuring and trusted.

Walter Cronkite speaks plainly, without pose or show. He has not had his head turned by success. He is pretty much the same Middlewesterner he started out to be, vastly experienced now to be sure, widely knowledgeable, continuously informed as are few of his countrymen, but still of, by and for the heartland of the United States of America.

A lot has been written about Walter Cronkite's personality, manner and appearance—his imperturable calm, friendly formality, exceptional credibility, businesslike delivery, and old-shoe easiness. Beneath or rather in addition to these qualities, this unflappable, good-natured broadcaster has also the capacity to be determined, competitive and entirely purposeful.

To think of Walter Cronkite's career is to go back inevitably to the time when you first met him no matter how long ago that was. For everyone who knows Walter understandably likes to think that their acquaintanceship reaches back a long way. In our case the span is a quarter century—almost an even twenty five years. . . .

It is the summer of 1946 and the place is Nuremberg. The ruins of the ancient Bavarian city lie within its bombed out walls. Hundreds of old buildings and dwellings with their overhanging gables, some of which had stood for nearly a thousand years, are no more. Piles of rubble line the narrow, twisting streets.

This is the historic city which Hitler defamed with his Nazi rallies and with his "Nuremberg laws." It is the community identified with the revocation of the citizenship of the Jews and with the decree making the swastika the flag of Germany. Its plight is a testimonial in destruction to the dead Fuehrer's insane conduct.

In the summer of 1946 there is something else that sets Nuremberg apart in the world, something else that makes it the focus of millions of eyes. Nuremberg is the scene of the war crimes trial of the Nazi high command. Goering and Hess, Rosenberg and von Ribbentrop, Keitel and Schacht, von Papen and Seyss-Inquart and the others are in the prisoners' dock as conspirators against humanity.

The case against twenty two of the top Nazis had begun in the preceding November. Some two months hence, on October 1, 1946, the four-nation court, presided over by Sir Geoffrey Lawrence of Great Britain, will sentence twelve to die by hanging, assign seven to prison terms and acquit three. But now in mid-summer, the trial is in progress. The French, British, Russian and American judges are on the bench. The prosecutors, including Justice Robert H. Jackson for the United States, are at their posts. The translators are in their booths, speaking into the earphones of the spectators.

Naturally the press of the world is there, too. And in the press corps is the chief correspondent for the United Press, already a seasoned reporter though only twenty nine years old. He is Walter Cronkite.

That post-war summer, H. Peter Hart and I, both officers in the United States Army, were stationed at nearby Altdorf, seat of the final consolidation of the several European editions of *The Stars and Stripes,* issuing strangely enough from the presses that had printed Nazi Julius Streicher's hate-mongering anti-Semitic *Der Stuermer.* From time to time, when in Nuremberg, either Peter or I would look in on the war crimes trials to see how things were going and perhaps to hear Justice Jackson or some other luminary of the prosecution make a strong presentation to the court.

Peter soon asked me if I had met the Cronkites. I think that Peter might have been attracted originally by Betsy Cronkite's pretty reddish hair, for I do remember that he remarked about the young wife who was helping her reporter husband. So I went to the United Press room in the press section; there I met this fellow Middlewesterner. Walter was a native Missourian, born in St. Joseph, and I was an Illinoisan, on military leave from the *St. Louis Post-Dispatch.* Right off we had plenty to exchange notes about.

For a reporter not yet thirty, Walter by then had seen an amazing amount of the action of those action-jammed years. He had joined the United Press in 1939, the year World War I flared into the open. After the attack on Pearl Harbor in 1941, Walter, young, energetic, eager, was counted into the United Press' plans for coverage of the war; come 1942 he reported the Battle of the North Atlantic. Then he went south with the Allied troops in 1943 to take part in the invasion of Africa. When the Normandy landings occurred in 1944, Walter was there with battle gear.

Dropping with the 101st Airborne Division out of the skies into Holland, he stayed with the fighting men month after month. When the Battle of the Bulge took place in the Dark December of 1944, he was with the Third U.S. Army. As General Patton's troops broke through the Nazi ring at Bastogne, Walter reported that welcome news to the home front.

Moving from hostilities to peace, Walter covered the Nazi surrender in Northwest Europe in June, 1945. Then he set to work getting the United Press active on a far broader scale in the coverage of Europe with bureaus and correspondents in the Netherlands, Belgium and Luxembourg. He had hardly more than laid out these lines for post-war reporting on the Continent when it was time to go to Nuremberg and follow the fate of the Nazis on trial before that unprecedented tribunal.

But let's flash back to Walter's "Show Me State" origin and account for his early years. Born on November 4, 1916, in St. Joe, as everyone in Missouri calls his home town, Walter was the only child of Dr. and Mrs. Walter Leland Cronkite. The father was a dentist with Dutch forebears. After schooling in Kansas City, he enrolled in 1933, in the midst of the Depression, at the University of Texas where he became a brother in Chi Phi but more significantly the *Houston Post's* campus correspondent.

He quickly found that he relished journalism and so welcomed an opportunity to join the Texas state capital staff of the *Houston Press* and the associated papers of the Scripps-Howard organization in Dallas, Austin, El Paso and elsewhere. Also he managed to find time to serve as a sports announcer for a radio station, a connection that was to lead to far more for him than he could possibly have dreamed.

After two years in academia, he forsook formal education in favor of the more exciting work of chasing news for the *Houston Post* fulltime. But the thrill of announcing news over radio pulled him back to the new communications medium and for a year he worked in radio in Kansas City. However, he was pulled both ways, and in 1939, disturbed because there was so much "show business" in and around radio, he moved back to wire news service work. For eleven years the United Press was his journalistic home.

Meantime he had been courting Mary Elizabeth Maxwell, a Kansas City newspaper staff writer who conducted a column captioned "Ask Hope Hudson." As one wag has said, Walter did. Their marriage took place on March 30, 1940 rather than earlier because he put it off until his salary had risen to $35 a week. Now the war came along with its overseas assignments and Walter and Betsy were separated for long stretches of time.

There must have been many occasions when he wondered whether he would ever see his most attractive wife again. To take one example, there was his arrival in Holland, already mentioned. The scary fact is that he crash-landed in a glider! John Reddy recalled the episode in *Television Age:*

"In that bitter engagement at Eindhoven, Cronkite and CBS correspondent Bill Downs were pinned down by machine-gun fire. As the attack intensified and night fell, the two became separated. Although the Germans were dropping anti-personnel bombs, Cronkite wandered through the dark, shell-torn woods, searching for Downs. Finally giving his friend up for dead, Cronkite made his way to Brussels. Haggard, dirty and shaken, he headed for the Metropole Hotel bar—and there found Downs, dapper in a fresh uniform, regaling a small crowd with a vivid account of his narrow escape.

"'I thought you had been killed!' the astonished Cronkite blurted. 'I walked through the woods calling your name!' Downs assured Walter that he had been equally concerned, but could hardly walk around calling his friend's name. 'If the Germans had heard me yelling 'Cronkite,' I'd probably be in a Berlin hospital now.' (*Krankheit* means 'sickness' in German.)"

Walter believed that there was only one way to cover World War II. That was for the correspondent to see it with his own eyes and thus to know firsthand as much of the time as possible about what he was writing. It was for that reason that he flew on eight bombing missions over Germany.

In going to Vietnam repeatedly and reporting direct to the American people, he has followed the same practice. But to tell that now would be getting ahead of the story. Following the war crimes trials in Nuremberg, he was assigned by the U.P. in 1946 to Moscow and for the next two years he covered the beginnings of the Cold War from that side of the Iron Curtain. He came back to the United States in 1948 to get into radio journalism; for two more years he reported Washington news for a group of radio stations in the Middlewest. Then in July, 1950 he signed up with the Columbia Broadcasting System to report the news in our national capital. That was twenty years ago and what two decades they have been—hardly less for Walter Cronkite than for the world!

In this span has come overseas transmission by space satellite. There has come eye-witness battlefield reporting by television that perhaps more than any other one factor awakened the American people to what they had been led into through the war in Southeast Asia. There has come live coverage of the cosmonauts' capsule flights to the surface of the moon and back.

If there were any question remaining as to the importance and influence of journalism by electronic media, it has been removed a thousand times over by the fantastic strides in the years that Walter Cronkite has been with CBS.

For he could be cited as a one-man proof of this all by himself. Besides being the anchor man on CBS Evening News, he has personally reported national political conventions and elections, inaugurations, coronations, the two Kennedy assassinations and that of Martin Luther King, the visit of Khruschev and the funeral of Churchill, the problems of race, of crime, of population, of the urban areas, pollution and unrest among youth, of welfare and health.

He has interviewed Presidents Truman, Eisenhower, Kennedy and Johnson. And he has been the means through which the views of such observers of public issues as Walter Lippmann have been more broadly disseminated than ever before.

Highly successful though Walter Cronkite's career has been—his income is in six figures—it has brought him disappointments and frustrations as well as satisfactions. After difficulties in the 1964 national political conventions, he was replaced by a team of news-casters. For a time it looked as if he might be on the way out. But he brought himself back, showing what television journalism could do best and winning new support by building new confidence.

Against his better judgment he once allowed himself to take on a commercially competitive morning show only to find himself surrounded by entertainment people who even provided him with lines! This bondage did not last long for he soon set about to free himself from so obnoxious a fate.

Many informed critics had their strong doubts when he appealed for the removal of radio and television from regulatory control by the Federal Communications Commission. Some rebutted head-on. But taken as a whole he has achieved a wide acceptance for his views. Instead of overclaiming, he recognizes the limitations of presenting news on a screen in a short few minutes. As he has said, in television "there are no back pages." Everything is on Page One. But he recognizes that the newspaper is here to stay, too, for it can do a great deal that television has not found a way to do and so far as is foreseeable never will be able to do.

Whether Walter Cronkite is "the single most convincing and authoritative figure in TV news," as *Time* magazine described him as long ago as October, 1966, an impressive series of awards, lectureships and recognitions goes far to make that superlative statement stand up. In 1969 he received the William Allen White Award for Journalistic Merit—never before given to a broadcast newsman—in recognition of the fact that his career of thirty years "has earned the admiration of the nation." Earlier the George Foster Peabody Television News Award in 1962 saluted, among other Cronkite achievements, his "Twentieth Century" broadcasts (1957-1966). The University of Texas, the University of Missouri, the University of Southern California, the Ohio State University, Syracuse University, Bucknell University and Rollins College all have cited him with honorary degrees.

The reasons for the esteem in which Walter Cronkite is held are amply evident in this collection of his addresses. "The

Journalist at Thermopolye," a lecture he gave at the Johns Hopkins University in 1967, must be the envy of every newspaper man who reads it. For it says what every reporter and editor should be proud to have said about the necessity of keeping the American people fully informed in the face of officials who attempt to cloak their self-serving acts in secrecy or through half truths.

Here are a half dozen quotations from the Hopkins lecture indicative of Cronkite's vigor and forthrightness:

"Merely rising up to defend our legal rights to free speech and press when it is under attack is not enough. We must take the offensive to clear away these encircling forces of untruth that are the real threat."

"The very facts of our nuclear age which has brought upon us this new problem of news management, demand that the public know more, not less, about the decisions of government and the men who make them."

"One of the reasons for the great confusion which wracks this nation over the Vietnam war is the fact that we were committed without a proper airing of the facts—all the facts."

"At the policy level, *silence* can be as misleading and as deadly a blow to truth and credibility as misstatement."

"The teach-ins and the student demonstrations served an important purpose in bringing home the fact that there was a large body of dissent and that there were some important and intelligent adherents to it."

"The reporters who exercise proper scepticism over the news from Washington are rendering a valuable public service and are in the long run helping Washington, not hindering."

"Loose talk can be controlled for a short while, but secrets have a way of eventually leaking and attempts to keep them by denying them to the American public through its press are foolhardy at least, fatal at worst."

Each of the addresses in this book invites quotation not once but many times. Each speaks pointedly to the challenges before our country and the world. Each suggests the heavy responsibility on the integrity and the intelligence of those who bring us our news day after day, especially the broadcast newsman on whom some sixty per cent of us are said to rely as a habit of life.

It is a temptation to tell more about Walter as a six-foot tall human being, as husband to Betsy and father of Nancy, Kathy and Walter Leland III; about his pleasures as a tennis player, sports car bug, sailing fan; and about the reasons for the legend and lore that have grown up about him.

Instead let's scoop the next collection of his addresses by quoting a bit of his speech before radio news executives in Denver on September 25, 1970. It deals with one of the more insidious of all developments in television and almost no one has been willing to come to grips with it. What Walter Cronkite said should have been in newspapers and on news broadcasts all over the country. Yet I saw it only in *Cervi's Weekly*. Here is what he said:

"Reliability is a handmaiden of integrity and I fear that many of us are not as careful as we might be to keep our escutchons unbesmirched.

"It is beyond me to understand how anyone can believe in, foster, support or force a newsman to read commercials.

"This is blasphemy of the worst form. A newsman is nothing if not believable. And how can he be believed when he delivers a news item if in the next breath he lends his face, his voice and his name to extolling in words the public knows he never wrote a product or service that the public knows he probably has never tested?

"When a newsman delivers a commercial he puts his reputation for honesty in the hands of an advertising copy writer and a client whose veracity is sorely tried by the need to make a buck.

"It is difficult if not impossible for the individual newsman who wants to protect his family to stand up to a management that demands that he indulge in this infamously degrading and destructive practice."

That is Walter Cronkite for you. Blunt, direct, telling it to the top exactly the way it should be told. Yet with compassion and understanding for the worker down in the ranks who is a victim of malpractice by management.

These pages are full of such criticisms and comments about communications in general, as well as insightful observations about the great challenges of our time. This book deserves wide reading, wide quotation, wide application. The convictions of our most trusted newsman deserve nothing less.

IRVING DILLIARD

CONTENTS

1

THE PROBLEMS WE FACE

It is not difficult to find analogies to the days just two-hundred years ago when Virginia's House of Burgesses met in Williamsburg to consider the crushing nature of the crown across the sea.

Our problems today seem far more complex than those that disturbed the colonists. Perhaps they are. If so, they demand even greater dedication, courage and resolve than the considerable quantities of these attributes displayed by the early patriots of Virginia.

As we plunge headlong toward the 21st Century, let us consider the inescapable crux of all the problems that are facing us.

How, with an exploding population and the increasing impingement of each of us on the other, and the necessity of meshing our lives for the greatest comfort of the greatest number, can we preserve the one characteristic without which life is worthless—the human dignity and the freedom of choice of the individual?

We must ask ourselves some hard questions. Have we, for instance, gone too far with civil liberty? A shocking question? Perhaps. But should we not permit ourselves—nay, should we not demand of ourselves—that we examine each question without the pre-conceptions that stifle honest research?

Address at Williamsburg, Virginia, February 3, 1968.

We can say to ourselves without embarrassing our democratic traditions: "Surely there is a way to protect the majority against the marauding bands of narcotic-crazed Hell's Angels without infringing on anyone's genuine civil rights, including theirs."

The Supreme Court takes action it believes correct in curtailing abuses of our civil liberties—but where are the original thinkers, the innovators, who can break with old tradition to find a modern answer to modern problems?

It is possible, for instance, that in the crowded conditions of the 20th Century man's civil liberties are going to have to be curtailed for the greater good of the greater number.

It is possible that freedom of individual action permissible when this nation was young and under-populated no longer is permissible as we enter middle-age and are over-populated.

These are radical thoughts, but we must not turn our backs on such problems, nor brand by unsavory names those who would pursue the research into them.

Some day, and the dawn of that day cannot long be held back, we must take a new look at state's rights, not because we believe any less in the principles on which the doctrine was conceived but because we realize that the nature of our nation is changing.

Our fiscal policy is in a shambles, partly because of unnecessary duplication of government. Taxes are duplicated and, what is worse, hidden in an attempt to deceive the people. Efficiency of government is impaired and the machinery overwhelmed by proliferation of government agencies, on both the federal and local levels.

Nor is this tendency restricted to government. Big business itself becomes burdensomely top-heavy as it expands, and the people pay a tax for inefficiency in the form of higher prices.

If it takes top-to-bottom re-structuring of the American system, then we should not be afraid of such radical re-building. That which is sacred in our past does not require lip-service to obsolence.

We need not so much states rights as human rights, and, of these, economic security and opportunity are high on the list. Without them discontent will fester in the land. But to provide them we cannot suppress ambition nor penalize success.

Place alongside states rights those of personal liberty and national sovereignty. No one desires to surrender any part of those achievements we hold dear and for which we have shed our nation's blood and wealth.

But let's not condemn the dissenters who feel that perhaps we have no choice in a world ever more crowded, moving at a speed which is ever increasing. When man learned to fly, he looked to the uncrowded skies to spread his wings and soar with the freedom of the birds. Today he finds himself restricted to air lanes and certain heights and landing patterns. The freedom he admired would bring tragic chaos.

It is not adequate to believe that the standards which were good enough for our fathers are good enough for us. The world, as much as we may deplore the fact, is not the same today as it was when the House of Burgesses met in 1768. As a matter of fact, it is not the same as it was just last year.

In 1940, which seemed turbulent to us at the time but which looks peacefully remote today, there were just 130 million of us. Today there are 200 million.

Where there were two of us trying to find a home, drive down the highway, find a secluded spot of beach, trying to buy a theater ticket—today there are three of us. In another twenty-eight years as we near the turn of the century there will be six of us seeking to occupy that same space that three of us occupy today.

When the founding patriots first sat in Williamsburg there were four persons per square mile in the thirteen colonies. Today there are 56 of us per square mile and by the year 2000 it will be 100 Americans per square mile.

Can we really believe that 1770 solutions are adequate for 1970 problems? If we are to meet our problems, the dissenters who speak revolutionary thoughts must not be stifled. They may have the answer to lead us from the wilderness.

We must dare to dissent from the old adages which have guided us. We must examine with a clinical eye the suppositions on which we have based our society. One of our wise modern philosophers, Marya Mannes, has put forth some of those propositions:

Money buys security. Well, does it? Against crime? Against pollution? Against corruption? Against congestion? Against addiction?

The pursuit of happiness is the great American dream. Whose happiness? Yours or theirs? Can the individual be happy in an unhappy society? Can he remain well in a sick one?

Welfare takes care of the poor. Does it? At what cost to us—and to them?

Democracy and capitalism are the pillars of a free society and therefore morally right. Right for whom? At what stage of development? In what part of the world? *Whose* morality?

Socialism and communism are morally evil and therefore threaten our existence. Why? Because their ideas are stronger than ours? Because they use force to promote themselves and we do not? Don't we? If we are both strong and morally right, what are we afraid of? These are questions we must ask, and the search for the answers should be unceasing.

A very keen observer of the scientific scene and a philosopher, Lord Ritchie Calder, notes that scientific revolution is the "replacement of one set of propositions that have served practitioners satisfactorily (in spite of anomalies) with a new set." A set of propositions, called a paradigm, provides model problems and solutions, the framework in which science works. He notes that to reject a paradigm—to foment *scientific revolution*—is to commit a "breach of accepted scientific tradition." Yet the great scientific discoverers have been revolutionaries. They have rejected an important paradigm of their discipline.

In political thought, in the discipline of the political sciences, we must be willing to escape our paradigm, we must listen to those who would escape, we must hear out the dissenters. We must seek out and make use of the original thinkers.

The Nuremberg trials of the Nazi war criminals were an excellent example of original thinking, although the motivation was suspect of revenge. Powerful arguments were made, and are still put forth, that such trials of crimes not previously set forth in international law, were ex post facto, and therefore themselves a crime against a basic principle of modern law—a legal paradigm.

Yet the counter-argument that prevailed represented innovation and a dissent from conformity, necessitated by the current need. It went that the world, in the atomic age, would not have a chance after a third world war to establish legal precedent against future offenders, that the judicial side of any new system of international law would have to establish its own precedent even before the legislative and executive sides of a future international system of order came into being.

The tragedy, of course, is that twenty-two years after Nuremberg the other parts of that international system are still but a gleam in our eyes, but that is not the fault of the jurists who have given us a body of precedent against war crimes when we grow wise enough to apply it.

Now today we find some who dissent from our current war raising the precedent of Nuremberg to claim the individual's rights to decide when war is justified. There is considerable question whether they have read well the documentation of Nuremberg and its findings, but there is a concept here that should not be lightly dismissed merely because it flies in the face of our conventional view of patriotism. It is dissent—and dissent must be given consideration no matter how revolting.

For, interestingly enough, "revolting" and "revolution" come from the same Latin word. And to be revolutionary in attacking our problems of today and tomorrow is not to *deny* our American heritage, the heritage of the patriots who once met here, but to *honor* it.

Indeed, to refuse to recognize the need for revolution is the ultimate denial of the principles for which the distinguished Virginia forefathers risked so much, offering even to lay down their lives.

We are now in a scientific revolution. In the life span of the youngest member of this audience we have sped through three eras—the atomic age, the computer age, the space age,—and now we stand on the threshold of the most revolutionary of them all, the DNA age—the unlocking of the very secret of life, of what makes us what we are. We soon will have the frightening knowledge of how to make man any way we want him—smart or stupid, tall or short, black or white.

In the next thirty years the transplant of human organs will be commonplace, the birthrate will be controlled, we will be exploring and perhaps colonizing the ocean floor. Can anyone deny that a political revolution will accompany that scientific revolution?

We have the future in our power. The 21st Century will not burst upon us in full flower. We can mold it to be what man wants it to be. But to do that we must know what we want, and we must examine each of our institutions to determine whether they stand up to the challenges of the century ahead.

We may have to look no further than our own failure to plan for this future to find the seeds of youth's discontent. Convinced that we are not doing the job, they are turning their backs upon up. And lest they reject that which is good of our institutions and that accumulated wisdom which we possess solely by reason of age, we must not reject these youthful dissenters. In youth's rebellion we must assist, not resist.

Society is going to change. The only question is whether we are going to help. Not short of death can we avoid being a part of the human parade. The question is: where will we be in it? Up toward the front, carrying the banner? Swept along somewhere in the middle? Or perhaps trampled underfoot as it marches over us en route to the future?

Our help is needed. While our way of life will change, we need to communicate, by word and deed, the values we know are constants—right or wrong, truth or falsehood, generosity or selfishness, dedication or cynicism, self-discipline or license.

The ferment aboard today in the land borders on anarchy, and there are fearful calls for law and order. But as surely as a boiling kettle will not stop generating steam just because a lid is clamped on it, our ferment cannot be suppressed by tanks and guns.

Far better than suppressing ferment, how about handling it the American way—how about channelling it toward a betterment and modernization of this society for the good of all? Why not use that steam to turn the lathes on which we can burnish away our self-doubts, polish our patriotism to a new brillance and fashion a new American spirit. But to do that we must listen to the dissenters. And we must begin now. There is no time to lose.

Only by opening our eyes and ears, our hearts and our minds can we arrest the trend toward turmoil, doubt, suspicion, frustration—but arrest it we must before a whole generation swept up by it, is asked by inevitable mortality to assume the mantle of leadership.

We are told that hippy children hate their parents because they have been given too much, because we have denied them the joys of struggle and so have denied them the sweetest fruit of all—the taste of victory. If this is our sin it should be viewed with compassion. We can be forgiven for failing to understand that we should pretend poverty to assure the right conditions of growth for off-spring. The sin is inherent in an affluent society.

But there is a solution which takes advantage of our material wealth. With this wealth and our technological advances we can free the new generation from the hours of toil once required merely to assure minimum sustenance.

We would substitute education—education, not just training that turns out cogs for the industrial machine. Education which would prepare them to meet the challenges of their time, the challenge to all humankind. We would make it possible for all men, freed from daily drudgery, to think, and to give public service.

We could inspire man to think of the problems, to seek solutions, to give of their new-found time freely and gladly. We might even earn their gratitude for giving them this guidance to the task ahead and for creating the environment that would bring forth a new nation to meet 21st Century problems with the same vigor, imagination and constructive use of dissent that did the first convention here in meeting the 19th Century's challenge.

And so we find again in our search for the future the thread to the past. For isn't this the core of the greatness of Virginia? Why were the men whose foresight we praise to this day so ominiscent? Because they were the educated men of their day, born and trained to public service. Yet in the economy of two centuries ago they were a small class.

What wonders we might accomplish in shaping the next century if a whole nation were educated, born and trained to public service! A nation of Jeffersons and Randolphs and Lees and Flemings and Carters and Henrys—is that really so wild a dream?

EDUC.

At 22, Thomas Jefferson stood outside the House of Burgesses and listened to Patrick Henry and, as Jefferson later wrote, he was inspired to read and ponder.

Presently youth is listening outside our doors but is it being inspired to ponder? Are we inspiring youth to turn off and turn away, or to come in and join the discussion of their future—and ours.

In his excellent book *Seat of Empire,* Carl Bridenbaugh says of the patriots who first met here: "Their equality and status questioned, even threatened, the now united gentry became radicals, gentlemen revolutionists. They revolted to preserve what they had."

If we are to preserve what we have we must lead or at least join the revolution. Let our new gentry become radicals and seek bold new solutions to our problems.

This country has not lost its ability to respond to challenge, and while the challenges of today seem frightening in their complexity, there is no reason for despair. The more and the greater the challenges, the greater the heroism of thought, deed and courage to surmount them—and the more exciting the prospect of the combat.

America can find sustenance and inspiration by looking again at not what we *were* but what we *are.*

2

TECHNOLOGICAL PROSPECTS

As we move into the future, the possibilities open to mankind stagger the imagination—in space exploration, medicine, education, the use of leisure, the environment in which we will live in our cities and homes. In the matter of technical hardware, it seems evident that mankind will excel. It's a pretty safe bet that our telephones, cars, washing machines and so forth will be more gleaming and efficient than today's.

But technology and science alone will not shape the future. Much more important is what we want the future to be like.

As a reporter responsible for a CBS News series called "The 21st Century", I've talked with many futurists—scientists, engineers, doctors, educators and other experts deeply involved in planning for the future. I'd like to talk about what I've learned from these men.

In the last 60 years it almost seems as if events have moved at a faster and faster pace. Today 25 percent of the people who ever lived on this planet are alive. By the year 2000 the figure will be 50 percent.

Today 90 percent of all the scientists who ever lived are alive and working.

In effect, we are just at the beginning of a science explosion—taking the first steps in the new technological age.

The Rand Corporation has a fascinating report on specific

Remarks to the Student Burgesses at Williamsburg Va., February 12, 1967.

breakthroughs in technology that might occur in the future. A hundred and fifty experts in all areas of science were asked to give their opinions of these breakthroughs and also when they might occur. Here are some of the results:

By 1975 we will have developed biological agents which will destroy an enemy's will to resist.

In another twenty years there will have been manned fly-bys of Mars and Venus.

In 1982 artificial plastic and electronic organs for humans will be commonplace.

The year after that we will have drugs to produce personality changes.

The experts see primitive forms of life created in the laboratory by 1989. And by the year 2000 there will be commercial transport by global ballistic missiles; and heredity defects will be controlled by altering genes.

Looking to the early part of the 21st Century these scientists see biochemicals aiding the growth of new organs and limbs, and drugs which will raise the level of intelligence.

By the middle of the 21st Century we will have learned to control the aging process, perhaps extending the life span by 50 years; we will be breeding intelligent animals for low grade labor, and we will have gained limited control over gravity.

But by that time some of these faintly unpleasant prospects will be your children's worry, not yours.

During my work on "The 21st Century" series I've had the pleasure of testing some of today's hardware of tomorrow—the vehicles with which we may explore the moon, the automatic cars in which we might ride to work, the research submarines that could take us to the ocean floor. I've skimmed across San Francisco Bay in a hovercraft, listened in on signals from outer space, eaten artificial foods and talked to scientists about what life will be like in just 33 years when the earth's population—now about three billion—will number *six* billion.

Now I'd like to talk about what we've learned about the problems and possibilities in five important areas: space exploration, oceanography, the future of the city and the home, transportation, and the future of medicine and genetics.

First, space exploration: the "space race" has become the "international Olympics" between the United States, the USSR, and France. One long range study indicates that the race into space will have reached the bounds of the solar system by the early 21st Century.

Men may get close views of Mars and Venus sometime around 1978. By 1985 the age-old mysteries of Mars probably will be solved when men land on the planet for the first time. Twenty or so years later it is expected that a permanent base will be established on Mars. Man will land on one of Jupiter's moons around 2021 and during that same year an instrument fly-by of Pluto will be possible—a trip to the edge of our solar system.

What will it be like to drive a lunar vehicle across the surface of the moon? Well, I can give you a pretty good idea. At Peconic, Long Island, Grumman Aircraft has built an artificial moonscape to test their "Mobile Base Simulator" or MOLAB, and they gave me a ride in it.

MOLAB is an electric four-wheel tractor-trailer with huge springy wheels, and an over-all length of about 30 feet. It is every bit as fantastic as the rest of the space program. The pressurized front cab has a dome with windows, instrument panel, controls and operating seats in front, and tapers toward the back where the living facilities are located. The trailer at the rear furnishes electric power to propel the vehicle.

In the 21st Century, as some men bounce around in strange lunar vehicles, establishing bases on the moon, other men will be exploring another region of our environment—the ocean. Although our oceans cover almost 70 percent of the earth's surface and contain potentially the greatest food and energy resource we have, they remain almost totally unexplored beneath the surface and only slightly tapped as a source of food and energy.

Jacques Yves Cousteau, the famous French oceanographer, envisions the day when modern biological science will be able to graft a gill onto the back of a man, making him completely amphibious. But until this comes about, if it ever does, pressure, light and maneuverability in thick metal bathyscaphes will continue to be major problems.

Probably the first material to be directly taken from sea water will, of course, be fresh water. New methods of desalinization, possibly using nuclear energy, will extract unwanted chemicals and impurities from the sea, or and hopefully, will answer the world's increasing need for fresh water during the next 35 years.

Recently, I took a trip to the ocean bottom in a research submarine, the Westinghouse Deepstar 4000. My underwater trip to the continental shelf, 2500 feet down, and 13 miles off San Diego, was disappointing in only one respect: there was none of the legendary undersea "jungle" about which so many have written. In fact, the spot we choose was as barren as a desert. Its barrenness can be overlooked, however, when you remember how much of the world's wealth—minerals, petroleum and foodstuffs—lie beneath the ocean. In the 21st Century, as never before, we will see a beginning to the yet-unheard-of deep sea mining and manufacturing industry.

So far I've briefly discussed how man might be learning to live in outer space and under the ocean. What about life in the city and individual home of the future?

By the year 2000, according to sociologist Kingsley Davis, one quarter of the world's population will live in cities of a hundred thousand or more. By 2050 the figure will be one half of the world population. At present rates of population expansion, it will take only a little over three hundred years for the whole land area of the world to become a single city.

A doubling of the world's population obviously doubles the need for food, energy and just plain space. Take a simple thing like water, for example. Today water needs in the United States are 515 billion gallons a year; by 2000 about 880 billion gallons will be needed. Some experts believe that by the end of the next 35 years exotic substances like titanium will not be our rarest resource. Instead we may find fresh-air to be of far greater scarcity and value.

If we are to achieve the glittering vision of urban life modeled in our World's Fairs, careful, thoughtful city planning will be necessary. Even as technology pushes man's personal vehicles three times the speed of sound, in the modern city he moves at an average rate of 9 miles per hour, the speed of the horse and buggy of 60 years ago; this in a shining machine that can cruise at 10 times that speed. Organization, clarity of design, social cooperation—all these are needed if modern cities are to avoid the stagnation of a gigantic traffic jam—of vehicles, of individuals and of ideas.

In filming one segment of the 21st Century series, I visited a full-sized mock-up of the living room of the future, made by Philco-Ford.

Computers have already found widespread use in business and industry, as well as in government. The next 35 years will bring their widespread use in the home. The "Space-Wife" of the 2001 A.D., might have a computer center in which she will be able to completely program her day's wifely chores. A push-button combined freezer and oven could completely cook a meal in 18 seconds with micro-wave heat. After a meal was finished, you wouldn't need a dishwasher. Plates would be molded on the spot for the meal and melted down again after the meal was over. Left-overs would be destroyed in the process.

The 21st Century home will be specially "air conditioned". Use of negative ions in the air could help us learn faster, feel better and perhaps, even get well quicker after surgery. Specially concocted air could conjure up invigorating mountain breezes or a balmy sea-shore atmosphere, with the flick of a switch.

Homes in the 21st Century probably won't increase in size, but they will become more functional. Along with color television, radio and picture phones, homes will come equipped with glowing wall panels and a typewritter computer console. The computer will make news, entertainment, business, education and domestic information available to the entire family. Different pieces of information will be presented simultaneously on electronic screens located throughout the house. Each house might have a robot maid controlled by a central computer, operated by a utility company.

Computers will not only share our homes with us, they may

help us drive our cars. In Detroit, I recently drove a car that was connected to a system that might be the first step toward automated driving. It is called DAIR (Driver Assistance, Instruction and Routing). The driver still does all the work, but he's assisted all the way by a computer and other driving aids.

With DAIR, when you want to take vacation trip, your gasoline company gives you a card that looks much like a credit card instead of a map marked with a heavy red line. Now in your car, down near the gearshift, is a device that looks very much like the receipt-writing gadgets that are used with credit cards. You simply push your card in, press a button, and you're ready to go.

As I drove the test car, DAIR navigated for me, telling me to go straight, turn left, turn right, and so on. How does it work? Its computer responds to magnets imbedded in the roadway.

Another part of the system is a dashboard display panel for road information. Traffic signs and signals, speed limits, and special hazards are flashed onto the panel by low-power transmitters along the road. For a real emergency, a voice override comes up and says, "caution, accident two miles ahead", "icy road", or "Ford license number such-and-such, call home immediately." A built-in telephone is also part of the DAIR system; you dial a coded emergency message which connects you with the police, garage, and so forth.

When one talks about transportation in the 21st Century, however, he has to include road-rail concepts such as the Alden Starr Car. The idea is that you'll have a vehicle you can drive around your town and yet hook into some sort of automated system when you get ready to go on a commuting run or a cross-country trip. And, at the other end, you can remove your car from the system and be free to drive.

For long-range trips in the 21st Century there will be supersonic transports and maybe even passenger rockets that could blast you to Tokyo in 45 minutes. On the ground there may be even more startling developments.

Research is being carried out in the development of "Ground Effects Machines"—hovercraft, as they are more commonly known. These are vehicles which use air pressure to suspend and propel themselves above any surface. Such a machine, ideally, could travel around the world—whooshing across land and water without stopping.

Today, plans have been proposed for an underground tube system connecting Washington, D. C., Philadelphia, New York and Boston. The full trip would take about 90 minutes.

The speed and glamour of future transportation possibilities seem shallow in contrast to the research I've seen in progress in biology labs and hospitals.

Aldous Huxley's book, *Brave New World*, opens in the fantastic setting of a hatchery for human beings. In one segment of the 21st Century series we have color motion pictures of just such a hatchery—as it looks today—a tiny human embryo viewed through the porthole of an artificial womb.

What was ominous fantasy 35 years ago is becoming fact. Professor Hermann Muller, Nobel Prize geneticist, has written: "Unless man shortsightedly destroys himself, as by means of radiation, he will literally remake himself." By working in functional alliance with our genes, says Muller, we may attain modes of thought and living that today seems "inconceivably god-like."

Dr. E. S. E. Hafex, an Egyptian-born experimental biologist at Washington State University, projects a fantastic possibility that pales even Huxley's *Brave New World.* In 10 to 15 years, speculates Hafex, it may be possible for a housewife to walk into a new kind of "commissary," look down a row of packets each carefully tagged, and pick her baby by label. The packets would contain quick-frozen embryos, each created to specific specifications.

Dr. Jonas Salk has warned: "The time has come, when the public must be made aware of the great impact of bioligical thought and knowledge. Such awareness, he goes on, will lead to further liberation of man and the flourishing of his great potential. But Salk says man also will be called upon to avoid the new dangers that liberation brings, and here, only his sense of values can be his guide.

Journeys into space may seem tame compared to another, more intimate realm man's explorations may take him into—the living cell. Already it is commonplace to keep alive various kinds of human cells in tissue cultures for extended periods of time, growing whole colonies from single cells again and again. Complete carrots have been "grown" with this method. Certainly, it's a long way from carrots to people, but work in the next 35 years may lead to the possibility of artificially constructing a *human* embryo.

[Without going as far as the creation of a whole new species, knowledge and control of genetics could bring about an end to hereditary disease or defects, or even control of "built-in" specific characteristics like hair color, sex or possibly degrees of intelligence.] "Genetic surgery," combined with refined techniques of artificial insemination and seminal storage, will bring about a complete revolution in our moral and social systems.

Probably the biggest medical breakthrough recently has

been with artificial organs and tissue transplants. For the first time, diseased or destroyed parts of the human body may soon be replaced almost as one would repair a watch. Doctors today are on the threshold of being able to literally rebuild parts of the human body. Today, for example, kidney transplants are relatively commonplace, and arterial grafts—made of Dacron—have been used with increasing success. A patient can order a silicon rubber tendon, a metal thigh bone, a finger joint or elbow joint; he can have installed a ceramic hip joint, an electronic bladder stimulator, a plastic eye, or trachea; nose or ear cartilage made from rubber, or a completely artificial Dacron heart.

Replaceable organs and genetic control are developments in progress today which may well reach fruition in the 21st Century.

"If man survives," concludes Cal Tech psychologist John Weir, "he can look forward to learning more about himself in the next 100 years than he has in the preceding *million.*"

To some students of social history, the transition through which we are passing at present is, in the perspective of human history, like the subliminal flick which marks the changing of a projected slide. A new world faces us even as the memory of the old continues to fill our mind. R. Buckminster Fuller dramatizes the changes which are propelling us toward the 21st Century when he says that "Man's first known circumnavigation of the earth is in a wooden sailing ship, around 1500. His second trip is by steel steamship in the mid-19th Century. His third is by aluminum airplane in the late 1930's. His fourth is a super-alloy rocket capsule in 1957. The times required for these circumnavigations—approximately three years by sailing ship; three months by steel steamship; three days by aluminum airplane and an hour by rocket capsule—clearly show that by 2000 A.D. almost anything you can dream of can and will have happened and that man will be living in an entirely new, responsibly conscious relationship to the universe."

The odds for tomorrow are not clear, but the 21st Century need not be an eclipse of human will and freedom as some thoughtful pessimists envision. Technology may not offer a world of fantastic delight, yet it also need not turn back and engulf its creators. Historian J. Bronowski looks ahead and faces the potentials of a new age and man's fear of the unknown, in these words: "What people fear is the reach, the power of technological discovery. And these people are not foolish: they recognize that nuclear energy, automation and biological advance are the most powerful forces of this century. But that power, he goes on, can be as great in peace as in war; we can use it to create the future, not murder it. Science promises a future in which men can lead intelligent and healthy lives . . . a future truly worth living for."

Good or evil are not inherent in machinery—they are inherent in man. So is the 21st Century.

3

CHANGE OR REVOLUTION

There are a lot of things wrong with this world we've made—poverty, ugliness, corruption, intolerance, waste of our resources, pollution of our air and water, urban sprawl, inefficient transportation, outmoded concepts of national sovereignty, the secret society of the establishment elite, the power of the military-industrial complex, the atomic race, the population explosion, war.

The mere fact that the species has survived so far seems hardly adequate cause for self-applause, nor can we indulge in self-congratulations for our civilization's considerable material and cultural development that has failed to guarantee survival or nurture the bodies and the spirit of all humankind.

If we are to survive and wipe out not only the symptoms but the causes of injustice and decay, there must be change. There is going to be change. This is inevitable. The question that the future asks: What kind of change—for the good or the bad, coming rapidly or more slowly, by radical excisement of the old, by amputation and transplant, or by mutation?

Some of our institutions have served us well; others have served us less than adequately because we have served them poorly. We can believe that we can improve our use of them,

Commencement address at Syracuse University, June 2, 1968.

and thus, bring about a more perfect society. Or we can believe that we must replace them with something new. One of the forms of change is, of course, evolution. The other is revolution, which may or may not be accompanied by violence.

The magnificence of the American system is that it provides for either or both revolution and evolution within its existing framework without the need for violent overthrow of the system itself. Violence not only thwarts the workings of the system but also impedes and distorts the revolution itself.

By transgressing the rights of the majority, violence is a denial of the very civil rights the revolutionists claim for themselves. It is intellectually intolerable that they should attempt to hide under the cloak of the very law, the very system they seek to destroy.

If the violence in our world today is a symptom of the illness against which the intellectual revolts, then consistency demands that he eschew violence in pursuing that revolt. Non-violent revolt *is* possible, and, indeed, may be desirable. John F. Kennedy and Martin Luther King, Jr. were non-violent revolutionaries. Both preached change, *within* the system, *within* the philosophy, *within* the dream. Their revolutions were to be in men's minds; their weapons, understanding, reason, sustained pressure to achieve their goals.

Their strategy was to conquer totally, yet bloodlessly; to win over the mind, and the heart. They hoped their revolutions would succeed quickly, but they knew they wouldn't. So they compromised, reluctantly but realistically, concentrating their revolutionary zeal on an effort to bring about evolutionary change. They knew, as another revolutionist, Thomas Lawrence—the Lawrence of Arabia—put it: "Progress is not made by the single genius, but by the common people. The genius raids, but the common people occupy and possess."

These men—the President who wanted to lead his nation into a new age, the civil-rights leader who wanted his nation to come of age; and the daring adventurer in seemingly another age—all saw that their revolutions needed pragmatism as well as idealism to succeed.

Today an entirely different kind of revolution is under way throughout the world. On both sides of the Iron Curtain young people are revolting against the Establishment.

Youth's discontent stems from the same impatience that has motivated each generation when it was young—impatience to get on with the obvious reforms that the Establishment seems reluctant to institute.

With the world's present potential for mass suicide with nuclear weapons and the apparent inability of the Establishment to control it, is there any wonder that the students of today rebel with an urgency unknown to earlier generations?

The Vietnam war goes on, human beings at the grim game of slaughter, while the diplomats plow their ponderous way in Paris. After a few thousand years of so-called civilization, it seems that there ought to be a better way. That, I suggest, is part of what young people are saying—there ought to be a better way.

Trying to draw a parallel between the rebels here and abroad isn't a fruitful exercise because the United States possesses to a unique degree the twin assets of democracy: the acceptance of dissent and the assurance of responsive, and, so far, responsible change. It is against these two elements that we must weigh today's rebellion in our country.

When does dissent go beyond the bounds of reasonable criticism and become a danger to the survival of the society that nurtured it? And if it does go that far, what should society do about it?

Our Constitution guarantees freedom of speech under the First Amendment. The courts remind us that this freedom is not unlimited, even if the Constitution says it is. "The abuses of freedom of speech," as Benjamin Franklin noted, "ought to be repressed." "But," he asked, "to whom are we to commit the power of doing it?" His question remains unanswered today after almost 200 years.

But if dissent applies to acts of conscience, as most of us seem to think it does, should society allow unlimited civil, or even criminal disobedience? If initial dissent does not produce a responsive change, say, in the conduct of a war, should we, as citizens, be entitled then to sabotage the war-efforts?

Speaking outside the court, Supreme Court Justice Abe Fortas declared recently that "civil disobedience is never justified in our nation when the law being violated is not itself the target of the protest." Furthermore, as he and others have argued, as long as the government Constitutionally protects the right to criticize, outright rebellion and wanton destruction can never be construed as legitimate dissent.

Some dissident student leaders argue that democracy does not exist for them at their universities; that their rebellion must be total, aimed at completely paralyzing and over-turning the existing leadership. They do not realize, or they choose to ignore, just how much freedom they possess today in the United States—which, despite some abuse, still compares favorably with that enjoyed by any other students in any other country, at this, or any other, time in history.

Furthermore, as Dr. Sidney Hook, of NYU's Department of Philosophy, points out: academic freedom is not, as many think, freedom of the students to learn what they please; it's freedom of the universities to decide what to teach, and how to teach it. *This* is the academic freedom that universities have been sheltering for many centuries—freedom *from* outside pressures, not freedom *for* inside pressure groups.

The freedom for which we all should be fighting is the freedom of free inquiry, the freedom to study our democratic institutions without fear of harrassment by misguided patriots, the freedom to advocate change without facing trial for heresy.

To determine what we keep, what we change, and what we discard, we must pursue full and open inquiry, which may require throwing off old concepts and shibboleths in the spirit of basic research.

4

POLITICS AND VIETNAM

If one seeks not tranquility but excitement, if one wishes not to sit by the side of a babbling brook but to be a spectator or participant in the moving and shaking of a world in transition, then this is a wonderful time to be alive—and better than almost any period in history of which I can think to be a reporter.

Never has the future been more in doubt nor has the challenge for leadership, and for the people, been greater. Each of the great nations, and for that matter the small, seems to be at its own crossroads, and collectively they all are at a cosmic crossroad. Russia either moves toward the comparative freedom of a benevolent socialism, not far removed from capitalism, or it moves back toward the prison state of communism; China, straining at her bonds, soon emerges as a friendly giant or a terrifying ogre; Western Europe moves toward the salvation of economic and political unity or splinters again into warring feifdoms; the emerging nations learn the value of cooperation or suffer the destructive competition of ancient city states. And America: All that one can find in the increasingly cloudy crystal ball is the certain image that we are at a fork in the road as well—either we take that road that leads to the spring from which we can refresh the Ameri-

Address at the Household Finance Corporation's Executive Conference, April 20 1968.

can spirit, or we take that other long road at the end of which lies the burial place of the American dream.

Our election this year will put us down one path or the other. There is yet time for the nation to regain prestige lost over the last decade of bluff, bluster and brinksmanship, to replenish the reservoirs of international and racial goodwill that were America's at the end of World War II, to restore the faith of the world's downtrodden that America *is* the land of the free and the brave, that here still lives the revolutionary spirit of independence. The choice of our next President will be the clue as to the course Americans wish to pursue.

Are we ready for the sacrifices required to experiment with new approaches to our domestic and international problems or do we believe the future can best be assured by preserving the economical, political and social structures that supported our past glories?

Perhaps never before have the fundamental issues that will affect the nation's vote been so volatile as they are this year. Vietnam, urban riots, inflation—these are exceedingly combustible issues.

Consider the confusion into which the entire political race was thrown by President Johnson's announcement on March 31st that he was offering a partial bombing pause to get peace talks started.

The two Democrats who had dared to challenge an incumbent President had done so primarily in disagreement with his Vietnam policy. Now they were suddenly stripped of their key issue and the shock showed in their first post-Johnson news conference. Richard Nixon on the Republican side, had his first major Vietnam policy speech ready for delivery the same night the President pre-empted the nation's attention.

Nixon wisely waited—and Johnson dropped the bombshell. Nixon's speech is still in his file cabinet.

Nelson Rockefeller's foreign policy advisors were drafting his Vietnam position paper the very night the President spoke. They went back to the drawing boards. Their efforts, like Nixon's and Kennedy's and McCarthy's, were somewhat stymied by a developing situation that could make any statement today look ridiculous tomorrow.

This—and the ensuing week's murder of Martin Luther King, Jr., with the violence it triggered—demonstrate the fluid nature of the issues on which the campaigns were based.

The President's Vietnam bombshell illustrated something else—the considerable advantages held by an incumbent President in an election year; the use of his position and power to influence events.

President Johnson surrendered only part of his power in his block-busting decision not to run again. Political power seeps away from a lame-duck office holder like water leaking from a punctured bowl, but his power to manipulate announcement or withholding of decisions, to initiate or delay policy shifts, to command television time and the public's attention—these are potent tools in an election year.

I believe that President Johnson's decision not to run was sincerely made. I don't think that any one of many contributing factors necessarily dominated the decision. Fatigue and perhaps a hidden concern about his health were perhaps contributing factors.

An unwillingness, perhaps only subconscious, to face defeat after winning the greatest popular majority in history, must have plagued the President. What a blow to anyone's ego it would be to have placed on the record such a drop in popularity in four years at the White House.

President Johnson thought that his action might win back some of this popularity, precious to him not just as a political commodity but to satisfy his complicated, sensitive ego. And he thought it would narrow what to him was the incredible credibility gap—a matter which worries him far more than he lets on in public and which he does not understand, which he thinks of as a "bum rap."

His decision was not a spur-of-the-moment thing. He considered making his announcement at the time of his State of the Union message to Congress early in the year but he was persuaded that, at that point, it would destroy any hope he had of regaining the cooperation of a recalcitrant Congress of which he had lost control in the 1966 election. His decision finally to take the big political step was part, I feel certain, of the whole thought-process that brought him to make the bigger step to seek peace talks with North Vietnam.

I have only sketchy facts on which to draw the following assumptions of what happened in the President's mind, but I believe them to be correct.

I believe that President Johnson was as shocked, perhaps more shocked, than were the American people by the Communists Tet offensive—that magnificently coordinated attack in February against the 35 largest cities of South Vietnam. I believe this brought to a head the President's growing doubts about the optimistic reports he had been getting for years from our military and political leaders in the field.

Those optimistic reports had told him we were winning in Vietnam, that North Vietnam infiltration was being severely limited by our bombings and search-and-destroy operations, that Vietcong recruitment was down and defections up, that their supply lines were disrupted and their morale low.

They had convinced him that the so-called pacification program to win the hearts and minds of the peasants and assure their security was succeeding. Their count of villages liberated and secured was soaring—making a certain chart of success in Vietnam.

They had encouraged him to ignore, as the blatherings of babes in the international woods, the critical reports of newsmen in the field in Vietnam.

They had not told him, because they themselves did not know, that the Communists had the potential, the capability, to mount a wide-scale offensive down the entire length of Vietnam and at what was believed to be its most secure areas.

This break-down in intelligence—indeed, this evidence that our intelligence was grossly inadequate—and, more important, this failure to understand the potential and the capability of the enemy, must have opened Mr. Johnson's eyes. It opened mine. When the Tet offensive began, I went out to Vietnam again. Up to then, although with considerable reservations regarding our bombing policy and certain other tactical decisions, I had believed we were pursuing the only course open to us there.

We may have made a mistake in our original commitment to Southeast Asia—or, at least, in the interpretation of that commitment—but once involved, once having placed our prestige at stake, once having lured our friends into the open with pledges of our unalterable commitment, I saw no alternative to continuing the fight until we had assured the security of South Vietnam. This was based on my last trip to Vietnam some two years before. I had seen nothing on that trip to fatally discourage me from accepting the optimism of the American and Vietnamese officials to whom I talked.

Then we were just building toward the 165,000 man force which we were told publicly was to be the limit of our commitment, although even then the one disturbing bit of evidence was that we were preparing the bases and filling the trans-Pacific pipe-line to take care of 400,000.

But I had reason to believe that the smaller force, along with a better-trained, better-equipped, better-motivated South Vietnam army, backed by a stable, honest government that had pledged to wipe out corruption—I believed all this could do the job. It might have, but none of the conditions was met. We continued to build up our forces and that triggered a greater response from North Vietnam so the ground war was escalated. The South Vietnamese army improved very little, if at all. The Ky government that began with such promise proved incapable of wiping out corruption or instituting the government reforms that alone could inspire the loyalty of the people.

And so in all the years we have been there, with all the blood and treasure we have spent there, despite all the optimistic statements of those who have a political stake in victory there, the Tet offensive proved that we were no closer to ultimate success.

The Vietcong did not win the Tet offensive against the cities. They did not achieve their principal objectives of creating a popular uprising and wide-scale defections in the South Vietnamese army or their ultimate pie-in-the-sky objective of bringing down the South Vietnamese government. On the other hand, they destroyed the myth of urban security, virtually destroyed the pacification program, forced wholesale redeployment of our forces, and caused such widespread property damage that years will be required to restore the economic situation.

History probably will call the Tet offensive a stand-off. According to "intercepts," captured documents and interrogation of prisoners, the third phase of the Communists' winter-spring offensive (the first phase was the attacks in the middle highlands in November and December of which Dak To was one battle, and Tet was the second phase) was to be a massive attack along a line south of the DMZ toward Quang Tri city, Hue and Danang.

On the political front, past performances give no confidence that the Vietnamese government can cope with its problems, compounded by recent attacks on the cities. It may not fall, it may hold on, but it probably won't show the dynamic qualities demanded of this young nation. Another standoff.

We have been too often disappointed by the optimism of the American leaders, both in Vietnam and Washington, to have faith any longer in the silver linings they find in the darkest clouds. They may be right, that Hanoi's winter-spring offensive has been forced by the Communist realization that they could not win the longer war of attrition, and that the Communists hope that any success in the offensive will improve their position for eventual negotiations.

This would improve their position and it would also require our realization, that we should have had all along, that any negotiations must be that—negotiations, not the dictation of peace terms. For it seems now more certain than ever that the bloody experience of Vietnam is to end in a stalemate. This summer's almost certain stand-off will either end in real give-and-take negotiations or terrible escalation. For every means we have to escalate, the enemy can match us. That applies to invasion of the North, the use of nuclear weapons, or the commitment of more American troops. And with each escalation, the world comes closer to the brink of cosmic disaster.

To say that we are closer to victory today is to believe, in the face of the evidence, the optimists who have been wrong in the past. To suggest we are on the edge of defeat is to yield to unreasonable pessimism. To say that we are mired in stalemate seems the only realistic, yet unsatisfactory, conclusion. On the off chance that military and political analyists are right, in the next few months we must test the enemy's intentions, in case this is indeed his last big gasp before negotiations. But it is increasingly clear to this reporter that the only rational way out then will be to negotiate, not as victors, but as an honorable people who lived up to their pledge to defend democracy and did the best they could.

BG It seems to me that this nation, far from losing prestige, could regain it by stating candidly and bluntly that we are unable to carry the burden of Southeast Asia alone any longer.

Why should we not put the onus for our predicament where it belongs—on our democratic allies in the world community? Why should we not say that we have done our best in manning this bastion for democracy and that we had reason to expect that others, for whom we were fighting the battle—and that is all the democracies—would join us in the good fight? Instead of their support we have had nothing but criticism and castigation. Men who call themselves leaders overseas have paid lip service to the cause but have not had the gumption or political strength to commit their nations' resources to the cause.

There is a strong case to be made that Vietnam has become too expensive, that not only is it draining resources sorely needed at home, but it is weakening this nation both in resources and resolve to meet communism elsewhere, in perhaps more vital corners of the world.

With our decision on Vietnam we also would put the world on notice that we no longer can afford to play the only policeman for democracy, that from here on out the police are going to have to be a true international force. The hope—and I think it is a not unreasonable one—would be that this shock treatment, far from dispersing the democratic forces, would bring them together in a rededication to truly mutual defense in which each participant and beneficiary plays his full role.

I do not suggest that any such grandiose scheme as this triggered the President's decision to seek peace talks. What his thoughts are on what we offer in negotiations and how we rationalize our policy shift, I have no idea. But I feel certain that his decision to limit the bombing to bring Hanoi to the peace table was based on the realization that we had reached a stalemate in Vietnam with no reasonable prospects of military victory. His decision not to run again was taken, I believe, to dramatize his break with the past. Further, I sense that his decision was taken without the approval of, or, at best, the grudging approval of, Secretary of State Rusk and the other hard-line advisers to whom the President has been listening.

Since almost immediately after the President's television address, Secretary Rusk, then in New Zealand, has been unrelenting in his pessimistic appraisal of the chances of such talks and it can be assumed that it has been his advice that has led to the serio-comic ballet over the site of the peace talks.

Much of the prestige and credibility advantage that the President gained through his March 31st offer is now draining away again as it turns out he didn't mean it when he said he would meet "anywhere anytime" with the North Vietnamese. It may be that he again is going to have to ignore his advisers and accept a less-than-perfect meeting place. Already there are indications that Averill Harriman and Cyrus Vance, in preparing for their roles as negotiators, are working far more independently of Secretary Rusk than might be expected . . .

The race for the Democratic nomination has turned into a magnificent scramble in which we have two declared participants—Robert F. Kennedy and Eugene McCarthy—and Humphrey. The Republican nomination looks like a bigger prize than ever and that has inspired renewed efforts by Nelson Rockefeller and Ronald Reagan, and that, too, will be a three-man race by August. We haven't had this much fun in years. And I can say that without any of that deep partisanship that thinks the country will go to hell in a handbasket if one or the other is elected. I know them rather well, from Kennedy on the left to Reagan on the right, and personally I like them all . . .

Whatever the results of this exciting race, America is going to profit. For this year, in contrast to 1964, there is the promise to full debate on the problems facing our nation and of the possible solution to them. In our democratic process, we can ask for nothing better than that.

5

BROADCASTING AND FREE SPEECH

I'd like to say a word about what's right with journalism—particularly in my chosen field of television and radio news.

We are under considerable attack at a time when we face another crisis of free speech and free press. This may not be the worst crisis in our recent history but it is a serious one. Those who feel threatened by freedom of speech again are on the march to stifle it.

I come to you today a little hurt and mighty angry at some of the charges leveled against broadcast journalism.

There is a fair portion of what we do that is not done well. There are things we are not doing which we ought to do. There are challenges which we have not yet fully met. Oh, we are a long way from perfection.

But much of the criticism levelled at us does not meet the criterion of objectivity. Some of it is just plain misinformed. Much of it is downright mischievous. I don't like the former and I have a very healthy fear of the latter. We are, of course, very young. Radio journalism is really a scant 35 years old. Television journalism is but 21.

We are the direct descendants of print journalism and, like the children of the privileged, we have had a head start in life. We inherited a great deal—a commitment to truth, integrity,

Address at the William Allen White School of Journalism, University of Kansas, March 24, 1969.

objectivity most of all—and we are trying to build on this invaluable legacy.

A great deal has been expected of us in our young years. As happens in many families, we are expected, it seems, to be a considerable improvement on the old man.

Newspaper critics complain that we interrupt our news programs with commercials. They seem not to have noticed the anachronistic makeup of their own newspapers that break a story in mid-paragraph to send the reader chasing through innumerable pages of ads on a hunt-and-seek for the remainder of the story.

Newspaper critics complain of TV sensationalism when their own papers banner the same stories and front-page pictures of the same events.

Newspaper critics seem to find something evil in what they call our "ratings battles," never noticing over their shoulders the great circulation battles when newspapering was not a monopoly.

Newspaper critics have complained of blandness in a television interview when their own newspapers were front-paging quotes from the same interview.

Newspaper critics note our rigid time limitations, somehow forgetting that the number of their news columns on a given day is dictated by the amount of advertising ordered, not on the amount of space needed to tell the day's events.

It is flattering that these critics expect us to be better than their own medium. Most of us are trying to oblige.

Some of today's harassment of TV news borders on the ludicrous, I submit. A Democratic Congressman from New York the other day complained that the network anchor men this year had enclosed booths overlooking the Presidential inauguration, while members of the Congress and government froze on the Capitol steps.

Congressman Otis Pike—a Princeton man at that—said there has been "a great decline in public acceptance of television news over the past few months" which may be inevitable because, "the demigods of communications sit in insulated, isolated comfort reporting to millions of Americans on happenings which they can neither hear, nor touch, nor taste, nor smell, nor feel."

I cannot speak for Chet or David but I, at least, plead guilty, in part. I did *hear* perfectly well and I *saw* very well, thanks to the places assigned to us for our inaugural coverage. But I must admit I did not touch, nor taste, nor smell, nor feel the 37th President of the United States. I'm not sure how I would have reported it if I had.

I am only chagrined if Congressman Pike touched, tasted, smelled, and felt the new President and we missed the story.

Some of the criticism of television news, it seems to me, beggars understanding.

Take this from Dr. Ralph Lowenstein, an associate professor at the University of Missouri School of Journalism: "TV has no tradition of objectivity," he writes. "Demands for TV objectivity are externally imposed through the 'equal time' and 'fairness' doctrine. These vague regulations—ordained by Congress and supposedly over-seen by the FCC—are regarded by the networks as restrictions on freedom of the press. Holding no moral allegiance to these two doctrines," he goes on, "the networks can violate them at will under the guise of news and public service programs."

"No tradition of objectivity." Can he really mean that? What does he and like-minded critics think the "networks" are—these ephemeral "theys" who have no tradition of objectivity?

The "networks" in the area where he addresses his criticism are the news staffs, and I respectfully submit that television newsmen are not a breed apart. Our motives and our principles of news integrity and objectivity are not different from those of newsmen of other media. Most of us are former newspaper and press service men; we went to the same schools as our colleagues in the print media; and we are ethnically, geographically, politically, and by religion, as diverse as they.

Lest by chance the Lowenstein school of critics is suggesting that it is the network management that has no tradition of objectivity, permit me an angry word on that.

Our network and station owners are no more nor less inspired by the profit motive than are the publishers of newspapers and magazines. I can testify that the executives of my network are far less meddlesome in the news process than the publishers for whom I've worked.

When the history of our branch of communications is written, the names of William Paley and Frank Stanton of CBS and David Sarnoff of NBC should loom large. They came to the ownership and management of the most powerful communications medium ever without journalistic background—just as have some publishers. But by their wisdom they have created one of the freest news systems yet. From the very early days of radio they kept the advertisers and the political power wielders off our backs until today we have established our independence and that tradition of objectivity Dr. Lowenstein fails to find.

Let me say a word here about advertising pressure which,

again, our newspaper critics seem to feel we suffer from more than do their publishers.

There is no question that the smaller the broadcasting station and the narrower the profit margin, even as with newspapers, the greater the leverage of the advertiser. And there undoubtedly are station owners, even as there are publishers, who bend here and there under the pressure.

But in my 18 years in broadcasting I have seen more and more station owners taking courage from their news editors, tasting the heady fruit of respect that can be won by the fearless conveyor of the truth.

Some years ago William Allen White wrote that "nothing fails so miserably as a cowardly newspaper." I suspect he spoke not only of commercial failure but of the greater failure, the failure to win the confidence of the people. A radio or television station also can fail this test of courage and when it does its owner wins not a community's respect and gratitude but its contempt.

All is not right in our world of television news. Our problems are immense. They are new, and they are unique.

A major problem is that imposed by the clock. In an entire half-hour news broadcast we speak only as many words as there are on two-thirds of one page of a standard newspaper. Clearly the structure demands tightness of writing and editing, and selection, unknown in any other form of journalism.

But look what we do within our time limits. Twenty items in an average newscast—some but a paragraph long, true, but all with the essential information to provide at least a guide to our world that day. Film clips that, in a way available to no other daily medium, introduce our viewers to the people and the places that make the news. Investigative reports—pocket documentaries—that expose weakness in our democratic fabric. (Not enough of those, but we're coming along.) Feature film reports that explore the by-ways of America and assure us that the whole world hasn't turned topsy-turvy. Graphics that in a few seconds communicate a great deal of information. Clearly labeled analysis, or commentary, on the news. I think that is quite a package.

The transient, evanescent quality of our medium—the appearance and disappearance of our words and pictures in almost the same instant of time—imposes another of our severe problems.

Most of us would agree that television's greatest asset is the ability to take the public to the scene—to the launch of a spaceship, a Congressional hearing, a political convention or a disaster. (In some cases these are not mutually exclusive.)

Live coverage of such continuing, developing events presents the radio-television newsman with a challenge unlike any faced by the print reported. The newspaper legman, rewrite man and editor meet the pressure of deadlines and must make hard decisions fast and accurately. But multiply their problems, their decisions, a thousand-fold and you scarcely have touched on the problems of the electronic journalist broadcasting live.

Even with the most intensive coverage it still is difficult and frequently impossible to get *all* the facts and get all of them straight even as a complex and occasionally violent story is breaking over and around one.

When our television reporter, in the midst of the riot or the floor demonstration or the disaster dictates his story, he is not talking to a rewrite man, but directly to the audience. There is no editor standing between him and the reader. He will make mistakes, but his quotient for accuracy must be high or he is not long for this world of electronic journalism. We demand a lot of these on-the-scene television reporters. I, for one, think they are delivering in magnificent fashion.

Our directors of an actuality broadcast, like newspapers' photo editors in a sense, have several pictures displayed on the monitors before them. But they, unlike their print counterparts, do not have ten minutes, or five, or even one minute to select the picture their audience will see. Their decision is made in seconds. Theirs is a totally new craft in journalism, but they have imbued it with all the professionalism, the sense of responsibility and integrity of the men of print. Mistakes? Of course they make them. But how few are the errors compared to the fielding chances!

Our profession is encumbered, even as it is liberated, by the tools of our trade. It is a miracle—this transmission of picture and voices through the air, this ability to take the whole world to the scene of a single event. But our tools still are somewhat gross.

Miniaturization and other developments eventually will solve our problem but for the moment our cameras and our lights and our tape trucks and even our microphones *are* obtrusive. It is probably true that their presence can alter an event, and it probably also is true that they alter it even more than the presence of reporters with pad and pencil, although we try to minimize our visibility. But I think we should not be too hasty in judging this as always a bad thing. It is not salutary that the government servant, the politician, the rioter, the miscreant know that he is operating in the full glare of publicity, that the whole world is watching?

Take, for instance, this matter of political conventions;

they have been a shambles of democratic malfunctioning since their inception. Printed reports through the years haven't had much effect in reforming them. But now that the voters have been taken to them by television, have sat through the sessions with the delegates, have seen the political establishment operate to suppress rather than develop the democratic dialogue, there is a stronger reform movement than ever before, and the chances of success seem brighter.

I would suggest that the same is true of the racial rioters and the student demonstrators, whatever the justice of the point they are trying to make. They use television—of course they do. Hasn't that always been the point of the demonstrator—to attract attention to his cause? But the *excesses* of the militants—whether on the ghetto streets or the nation's campuses—as shown by television with almost boring repetition—tend to repel rather than enlist support, and this is a lesson I hope and *believe* that rational leaders are learning.

America will not be divided by *more* exposure of the dissidents, but by less. It is not pleasant to look up the excesses of the militants of whatever cause, but far more unpleasant would be the consequences of denying them access to television and the public hearing it provides. Yet there are those today, some in high places, who would do that very thing.

Down through the years of the William Allen White lecture series there have been frequent, almost annual, references to attacks against the freedom of press. The Establishment of whatever age, whatever year has been chary of its critics. In times of extreme stress it has sought to muzzle them.

While, at least since the American revolution, the Establishment has paid lip-service to freedom of speech and press, there seems to be an unexpressed desire to limit this freedom to the establishment itself.

The Establishment works, subconsciously, on the autocratic philosophy that it knows what is best for the nation and the people. It needs for its own purposes of leadership—in commerce and in government—a free flow of information so long as that information, when it is disturbing, is not shared with the people.

The press in the early days after the invention of movable type was looked upon with considerable fear and suspicion, but when the Establishment realized that only the wealthy and privileged could read anyway, its worries were eased.

More people read today, but unfortunately a vast number do not read very well or very thoroughly. Television and radio now are reaching the poor, the uneducated, the underprivileged, and the establishment's worries again are threatening freedom of information.

Our immediate crisis stems directly from the fact that we, in networks news, are, indeed, politically independent, uncommitted and open-minded, responsible only to the principle of honest reporting. We are not affiliated with any special interest and we are not addressing a "like-minded group" but people in the mass. In taking the middle of the road, we are sniping from the sides.

Remember the clenched fists raised against us at the Republican convention of 1964? Four years later it is the Democratic Establishment that shakes in anger that we dared to report as it was their clam-bake at Chicago.

How much easier is would be to take a side and enjoy the security of being among friends!

No one is going to try to take our freedom in one big

gulp. The enemies of free speech will try to nibble us to death. And don't underestimate them. With a sense of the jugular, they know they are likely to be successful only if they can divide the press and TV. They'll nibble us in TV news until we're gone. Then they'll turn their attention again to the press.

The heat is off the press right now and it's on TV. But a newspaper editor would have to be of incredibly short memory to rest easy with this temporary state of things.

He would have to forget the nibbles of yesterday. He would have to forget the Congressional demands for investigations of press bias that followed the 1952 election, or the recurring suggestions during the forties and fifties for licensing of journalists. So seriously was that proposition being considered back in 1952 that Erwin Canham felt called upon to condemn it from the same platform on which I am making this speech.

The press is made up of a collection of individualists and some mighty cantankerous ones at that, but it closes ranks when its freedom is threatened. I don't think it has fought back enough in some cases—for instance, against news management in government agencies, against State Department clamps on the free movement of correspondents abroad, against Bar Association dictates on freedom of information. But it does move to the barricades to meet the assaults on a free press.

I would be much surprised and greatly saddened if we of broadcast journalism did not join the press to a man at those barricades. And yet today we find newspapermen of uncertain mind and divided loyalties regarding the threat to broadcasting freedom.

There are some who seem to believe that a little government

control of broadcast news might be a good idea. Can they really believe that we can exist as a major communication medium half-free—or, perhaps, do they not want us to exist as major competition? I think that group, as small as I hope it is, should do some soul-searching.

Perhaps its members simply are unaware of the odious nature of the harassment from Washington—the Federal Communication Commission's assumed right to ask us to explain our news coverage, and giving us twenty days to document our case; the attacks by Congressmen and Senators who are scheduling investigations with a view to further regulating us, a Presidential commission demanding our testimony on how we have and will cover the nation's turmoil of violence, FBI agents assigned to a Congressional committee interviewing people across the country who appeared in our "Hunger in America" broadcast.

Should different rules, different criteria exist for the press on one hand and radio and television on the other? If the answer is "no," then we have a right to ask those who would muzzle radio and TV if they also would muzzle the press. If the answer is "yes," then we have a right to ask *why* there should be different criteria. Is it because we are less responsible and, if so, by whose standards—or because perhaps we are more powerful?

Those who would hobble us believe they have the instrument at hand in the licensing of radio and television stations. Their rationale is that we who broadcast are using the people's air and that the people—that is, the government—have the right to say what goes on it. I challenge that doctrine as outmoded and archaic, dictated by circumstances that no longer exist.

In the early days of television, as in radio, there were only a limited number of channels available for commercial broadcasting. It was necessary for somebody, and it logically was the government, to allocate those channels. The law that gave the government that authority said only that the stations so licensed would operate in the "public interest, convenience and necessity." That law specifically forbade government censorship by the regulating agency, but the Federal Communications Commission has assumed the right to examine a station's programming and to require a certain portion of time to be allotted to so-called public affairs programming in fulfillment, presumably, of the "public interest" stipulation in the law.

But since that law's inception, thanks to the opening of the ultra-high frequencies in television and the FM band in radio, scores of additional channels have become available.

Already there are more radio and television stations than there are newspapers. It is the rare city that is not served by more television stations than by newspapers, and by infinitely more radio stations.

There are more one-newspaper cities than there are one-television cities. There are more television networks serving radio and television stations than there are news agencies serving the newspapers. And yet there are still *more* channels available for the bidding on UHF and FM.

It is cheaper to start a television station than a newspaper. It would be easier economically for a group with a cause—public education, art, political propaganda or simply profit—to get into broadcasting than into publishing.

Thus it would seem that the government's reason for being in the business of controlling what goes onto the people's air, because that air is limited, is no longer valid. It is clearly a restriction on free speech for the government to retain that control after the necessity for it has passed. Control over what is said on the people's air should be vested in the people's good sense to accept or reject what is said, the ultimate freedom of choice.

That television should respect the legal restraints against libel, slander and salaciousness is assumed. It also is assumed that the government still would have to allocate the channels but on a first-come first-served basis, without the imposition of a bureaucrat's standards of news judgment, good taste or political security.

My proposals here have no stamp of approval from anyone, as far as I know. They are radical. There are vested interests in my own industry—in television, that is—that I am sure would not like to see the status quo upset. There certainly are those outside the industry who believe the government must dictate television programming practices for the people's good.

Ideally we *would* have a system of totally free broadcasting stations—free from commercial control, free from government control, free from foundation control, free from all political, social and economic pressures.

Such an ideal station would be an electronic Union Square or Hyde Park corner, providing a soap box for anyone who could make it to the studio.

But this is Utopia. *Someone* would have to pay the upkeep; *someone* would have to allocate the available air time; and we would be right back to control, by one establishment, one group, one political philosophy or another.

No; far better than that imperfect stretch for the ideal is

the freedom of competition that has served us reasonably well so far in preserving our freedom of information.

Our experience in publishing in this nation guarantees that we can safely take our chances with *laissez-faire* broadcasting, that broadcasting entrepreneurs will provide a varied diet, a diet for each taste even as today, motion picture producers and book publishers offer products that run the gamut from the obscene to the glorious.

I do not doubt that, freed from the governmental requirement for public service, some broadcasters would drop all news from their schedules and become nothing but electronic movie exhibitors.

It would be better if broadcasters with that inclination got out of the news business anyway. The way would then be clear for the broadcaster who had a genuine desire for community service (and there are, and would be, many), his desire buttressed by the certainty that good, thorough, trustworthy, independent news programming also can be profitable.

I trust that the generation of newsmen already is here that dreams of having a good country television station just as we used to dream of a good country newspaper. Economically it is going to be possible.

Whether or not we in broadcast journalism succeed in striking off all the government restrictions that shackle us, it is important that we prevent any more from being clamped on. It is important that we establish once and for all that the First Amendment guarantee of freedom is as applicable to broadcasting as it is to the press. It is important that all branches of government—Congress and commissions—know that they have no more right to call us to account for our news judgment than they have to call to account the newspaper man; *ex post facto* examination of our judgment is a serious harassment that makes a mockery of press freedom. And it is important that the press join us in recognizing that a threat against the freedom of one newsman, whatever his medium, is a threat against all.

It is clearly essential that all of us journalists join in the most important phase of our mutual battle—to convince the people that our fight for freedom of the press and speech is not a self-serving struggle but is in defence of their right to know. We are their eyes and their ears. To blind and to mute us is to blind and deafen them, and a democracy cannot survive with a people so handicapped.

I said at the beginning of this talk, and I say again at the end: This business of broadcasting the news is not perfect. It is no more perfect than newspapering. It is never going to be perfect. But we who are in it are going to continue our efforts to make it as nearly perfect as we can.

There are and there will be moments when the problems seem insurmountable, the challenges unmeetable; when we are beset by self-doubts. In those moments we shall cling to one certainty which shall sustain us. And that is that we are all professional journalists dedicated to truth, honesty, to telling it as it is without fear or favor—and that there is no politician or bureaucrat who can make that claim.

6

COVERING POLITICAL CONVENTIONS

I don't recall ever hearing whether a tempest in a teapot ruins the tea therein. I imagine it does not.

It seems to me that the criticism of television's coverage of the political conventions, particularly the Democratic proceedings in Chicago, is a tempest in a teapot. And I don't think the tempest has ruined the product—the news coverage of those events.

After the Republican convention at Miami Beach there were suggestions that television should look anew at these quadrennial clambakes, that they obviously were far too dull to warrant gavel-to-gavel coverage. We haven't heard that criticism of the Democratic affair.

Since Chicago all sorts of newspaper editorialists, columnists, politicians and a few thousand citizens have suggested that television should review its procedures to improve its coverage of political conventions. We have been accused of being biased, unfair, one-sided, prejudiced, hysterical, rude, inconsiderate—among other things. In my case, the accusations included one leveled by a columnist I respect that I was "inexplicably obsequious" in interviewing Mayor Daley.

The more specific of these charges can be answered with facts and figures. At CBS News a detailed study of the tapes

Remarks on April 10, 1969.

and transcripts of our broadcasts by some editors and executives noted for their eagle eyes and fault-finding ways has convinced them that we discharged our journalistic responsibility with fairness and objectivity.

These are hardly impartial judges, you say—the accused acting as his own jury. True, but the detailed examination of our coverage of the Democratic convention and its ancillary madness shows that we gave the speeches and business of the convention as much time or more than in previous years and thus the dissenters and provocateurs had no more time than they have had previously, they just perhaps were more articulate and cohesive; that we frequently covered the show and talk of the provocation of the dissenters who eventually were the victims of police brutality; that we did report on police as well as civilian casualities in that action; that we did give Mayor Daley his chance to answer his critics; that our analysts and floor reporters did, indeed, balance their comments on the Chicago happenings.

All news media have come under some degree of attack since Chicago, but the larger share of attention and the more strident charges have been devoted to television.

Some critics in and out of government have suggested that television newsmen need to do a little "soul searching" or more drastically, that the government should more stringently control and regulate what goes on the air. Humbug and balderdash!

While I can speak only from my own experience of eighteen years at CBS (and fifteen years of newspapering before that) and I do not get an opportunity to see the other networks' convention product, I don't acknowledge that our motives or principles need one moment's attention. I *know* them to be of the highest.

If there are others who suspect our motives, let them have their inquiry. Although I suspect political motivation on many of their parts, with a little self-serving thrown in as in the case of the print media, some of our antagonists may honestly believe there was a conspiracy by television to distort the convention proceedings or to influence them.

Few of our critics, I am certain, would wish to indulge in a witch hunt or a fishing expedition so I trust that before pursuing their shotgun criticism they would attempt to back their suspicions with an indictment containing detailed and specific allegations. Before they reach that point, I submit, their emotionalism will have been considerably dampened by the facts.

One fact they should be able to establish quite easily is that television newsmen are not a breed apart. Their "motives and principles" are not different from those of newsmen for other media. Most of us are former newspaper and press service men. We went to the same schools as our colleagues in the print media. We are ethnically, geographically, politically and by religion as diverse as they.

Our network and station owners are no more nor less inspired by the profit motive of a free society than are the publishers of newspapers and magazines and from past experience I can testify that the executives of my network are far less meddlesome in the news process than the publishers for whom I've worked.

Why then is television singled out for criticism? For several reasons, I suggest:

(1) Television's considerably greater impact than any other news medium. Millions of viewers watched our cover-

age of the Chicago convention and its violent and unfortunate sideshow.

While I can't statistically prove the assertion, I would be willing to bet that the large majority of our viewers *heard* far more words spoken by television reporters and the news subjects than they read in their newspapers.

Television thus is the natural target of whatever frustrations the publishers or newspapers feel regarding the convention coverage. Except for the most avid readers of the dailies, the public got most of its information from the television screen. Further, the America people saw the events played out before them and there can be no question about the greater impact of that first-hand experience.

(2) The inherent problem of "selective" viewing of television.

A large percentage of our viewers do not see all of our coverage. Natural limitations dictate that they see only selected sections of the coverage. They might see the report of police brutality at the Hilton Hotel and miss Mayor Daley's explanation of it (which, incidentally, occupied more of CBS News air time than the incident itself.) Or those who criticized my interview of Daley as being too bland may well have missed my stated intentions, in the interest of fair and honest journalism, to give the Mayor a chance to answer his critics.

It obviously is impossible to present all sides of any controversy simultaneously. Even a newspaper can't do that, and has to present the many facets in different paragraphs, frequently on different pages. But at least with the print media *most* of the arguments can be presented in the same issue. Television's presentation of opposite sides may have to be many minutes or many hours, perhaps even days, apart and there are bound to be many viewers who miss one side or the other.

The broadcast of a developing news story also obviously places severe restrictions on the reporters and editors. Even with the most intensive coverage it still is difficult and frequently impossible to get all the facts and get all of them straight even as the story is breaking over and around one.

Try as hard as we might to recapitulate later with the fuller and possibly more accurate explanation, we are bound to miss some of the original viewers.

(Incidentally, sometimes fact never quite catches up with even the most astute newspaperman. A distinguished editor and columnist the week after the Chicago convention was still reporting that "some" Chicago policemen were injured "critically" in the rioting. The official Chicago report on the demonstrations listed no critical injuries to police or rioters.)

(3) The strange phenomenon of image transferal.

Large numbers of our viewers quite clearly confuse our reporting of an event itself.

Even as we were accused of fomenting the confusion in the Dallas courthouse basement that day of the Lee Oswald shooting, by those who forgot the confusion surrounding the Lindbergh kidnapping before the days of TV, we today are reaping the blame for convention disorder that long preceded the advent of our electronic pencils.

Still photographers and the writing press are equally guilty of contributing to the confusion. They did so long before television—note the Lindberg kidnapping chaos as just one example—but no one *showed* them plying their trade before.

We are *showing* the convention, and perhaps in some small measure we are contributing to it merely by our presence.

But we aren't manufacturing it out of whole cloth.

As far as the conventions go, the answer clearly is in the reform of the convention procedures themselves. And in this regard I return to my often-stated and frequently criticized suggestion that it is not necessary that we be admitted to the actual floor of the convention, that there is a better way (such as the use of immediate off-floor interview booths) to cover the non-podium action in order to permit a more orderly convention procedure. But those are matters of technique, not of motive or principle or news judgment.

(4) The *assumption* that the airwaves belong to the people and that they therefore have a right to control the news broadcast on them.

In the early days of television (as in radio) there were only a limited number of channels available for commercial broadcasting. It was necessary for somebody, and it turned-out to be the government, to allocate those channels.

The law that gave the government that authority said only that the situations so licensed would operate in the "public interest, convenience and necessity." That law specifically forbade government censorship by the regulating agency.

Since that time, thanks to the opening of the ultra-high frequencies in television and the FM band in radio, scores of additional channels are available and today the only factor that really limits the number of stations in any given market are the economics of that market.

Just as economics have eliminated newspaper competition in most of the nation's cities and created monopoly newspapers, economics limit the number of television stations. And the fact is that it is a rare city today that is not served by more television stations than by newspapers.

Again it is only economics that limits the number of television networks. And, incidentally, there are more television networks servicing the television stations today than there are full-time domestic wire services available to the nation's newspapers.

There is no more reason to believe that the television station owners or the network operators are single-mindedly attempting to control the news than there is to believe that the newspaper owners and the wire services are trying to control it.

Not only is there such a disparity of viewpoints among the station and network owners as to make such conspiracy impossible, but there is the ever-present and healthy competition between networks and between television and print as to make such conspiracy unlikely.

Other than conspiracy, it seems that the other charges against us must all come under one heading—news judgment.

It is futile to investigate or explain this highly subjective function. No two writers, editors, producers, network presidents or newspaper publishers will agree on the exact shadings of news treatment. Certainly no two politicians on a regulatory agency are likely to agree.

No inquiry can legitimately investigate our news judgment, nor what we choose or do not choose to show, nor what we choose to say. Ex post facto examination of such matters is as serious a threat to an infringement of the press as is censorship itself for it implies our responsibility to a higher authority. Those who want to impose that higher authority are asking for censorship and control of an important news medium. If that is acceptable for television today, doesn't the turn of the newspapers come tomorrow? And what is left then of free speech and a free press?

Self-examination, constant re-appraisal of methods and techniques is incumbent on any business or profession. We in television need to study, as we have after every convention and election, ways to do our job better.

And that means to explore means of doing a fairer job, to reach toward the probably impossible ultimate of total fairness and impartiality free of any preconceptions or prejudices (including those dearly held ones regarding freedom of press, speech and journalistic enterprise.) This is our responsibilty, and we are discharging it.

In a Senate speech the other day Senator Gale McGee of Wyoming, suggested that television could "serve a noble cause by raising the political sophistication of our people." Is it not possible that what has so galled and frightened the politicians is that we have, not only through convention coverage but through our daily broadcasts and our many specials, already raised that "sophistication"?

The demand for more democratic procedures, for reform or abolition of the conventions themselves, have come not from television but from political leaders. And these political leaders have reflected a popular demand that most probably has been inspired by television's exposure of the inequities and inanities of our present system.

We didn't make those inequities and inanities. We merely displayed them for all to see. It is a dangerous fallacy to believe that our ills can be cured by executing those who report them.

7

THE INFLUENCE OF ADVERTISERS

I don't have anything against advertisers. As a matter of fact, some of my best friends are advertisers. Oh, I'm not perverted about it. I don't automatically love a person just because he or she is an advertiser.

Advertisers are a great comfort to a broadcaster. I've always thought it would be mighty traumatic sitting there at the Public Broadcast Laboratory, broadcasting away with never a commercial interruption. Actually the commercials are something of a plus—besides their income—on our evening news broadcast. Just when the viewer has been convinced by me that things couldn't be worse, the commercial proves that they could. Or, conversely, provides comic relief.

I don't even mind the interruptions by the commercials. Besides the pleasant tinkle of cash dropping into the collection plate, commercial placement within the news broadcast, provide us with a convenient point to end one series of interconnected items and move on to another—to move without an inelegant segue from tragedy to something less solemn, for instance . . .

Myths die hard, and one of the myths that persists about our business is that advertisers attempt to control or influence what we say and how we say it. Or that we are responsive to

Address before the Association of Industrial Advertisers, New York City, May 5, 1969.

sponsor eyebrow-raising and censor ourselves in order to attract or keep advertisers.

The remarkable thing is that in a short time, relatively, the best broadcast news organizations have established a total independence from advertisers. The wall between sales and news content, at least in our shop, is quite impregnable. Advertisers have no rights of approval, no rights of review. Our journalistic independence of advertisers is a good deal greater than exists in many magazines and most newspapers.

But the truly remarkable thing is not our own insistence on independence—but that advertisers have come to accept this independence in broadcast journalism. Whatever difficulties we might have with others in maintaining our integrity and independence, it is an immense tribute to advertisers in general that they accept, and even embrace, this fundamental character of journalism. I cannot recall in recent years a single example of even the most subtle attempt by an advertiser, or a prospective advertiser, to breach the wall of our journalistic independence and integrity.

I doubt that any network—or perhaps any news organization—has more persistently, over the years, dealt with the problem of cigarette smoking. We did our first radio documentary on the subject fifteen years ago, our first TV documentary six or seven years ago. And yet the cigarette people, who I understand account for perhaps ten percent of the advertising on the CBS television network, have never approached us at CBS News to try to coerce us or discourage us in our reporting.

We have reported accurately and fairly action by the Federal Trade Commission and the Food and Drug Administration against some of our advertisers. We did not pull our punches on auto safety. We have reflected public concern about the gas station give-aways.

What has been achieved is practically a journalistic ideal—recognition that our job is to report news, the advertisers' job is to sell his product, and never the twain shall meet.

And yet while so many people have been looking under the bed to find the non-existent advertising intruder, the room has very visibly been invaded by the federal government . . .

Political transgression and coercion has been amply evident of late. If politicians do not like our convention coverage, or our treatment of poverty in Marks, Mississippi, or hunger in San Antonio, Texas, the Federal Communications Commission, responsive to Congressional and editorial pressures, demands explanation. Some Senators want to license networks so that they can get at the handling of news. And some members of Congress propose to invade our reporters' notebooks by requiring us to hold for six months all our film and tape which we have *not* broadcast but have edited out—which must mean that someone ought to review our news judgments. Or they hold Congressional hearings to determine why there is violence and what causes riots. And it is suggested that violence and riots might go away if only we did not report them. In effect, is is proposed that we apply not news judgment, but deistic decision to conform to the standards of the status quo. Every dictatorship from Czar Nicholas to Castro has operated on that principle.

As long as broadcasting is regulated by the federal government it cannot be free, and there are always going to be some—owners or news managers or newsmen themselves—who are going to report and edit with one fearful eye on big brother in Washington.

8

THE JOURNALIST AT THERMOPOLYE

Seldom in the annals of lecturedom has there been so corny a title as that prefixed to my address. However, in its essence it is not entirely without its own inner meaning, for one of those aspects of courage to which a newsman should be dedicated is the bravery it requires to reject the easy cliche, the trite phrase. By picking this title, I have exposed the proof of my own fallibility.

Since at least World War I each generation has been more cynical than the last. The belief in old values slips away faster than we can replace them with adequate substitutes. Our faith in our fellow man fades and is replaced with doubt and distrust.

Honesty has become old-fashioned and the very use of the word subjects its user to that gutteral "ich" that is the younger generations' Bronx cheer.

This is not just a moral or philosophic problem. I think it has grown to the proportions that today it is a real, an immediate problem that could directly affect our ability to survive. The democratic system is built on honesty and the belief in the honesty of our fellow men.

We—all of us, the nation and its press—today stand at a Thermopolye which is not that Grecian pass where the Spartans stood but the gap at which our credibility rests.

Frank R. Kent Lecture at Johns Hopkins University, February 9, 1967.

Today truth and honesty are surrounded by untruth and dishonesty, by dissembling and distortion, by cynicism and disbelief. Through apathy and unnecessary hopelessness, we can lose to these black forces the great bastion of mutual confidence that is the guardian of our democracy.

I believe this to be a forum for discussion of this problem. For the matter to which I address myself is not one alone of freedom of the press. It applies as well to academic freedom, to political freedom, and to all those freedoms which are essential if man is to speak, to write, to act out and to believe the truth.

Yale University's Provost, Kingman Brewster, Jr., addressing a gathering of journalists for the *Hartford Courant's* 200th anniversary dinner a couple of years ago, put it this way:

"Your institution and mine are clothed in the peculiar privileges and immunities of a great tradition. Even your owners, even my trustees; even your advertisers and my alumni; even your readers and my students know that conscientious exercise of freedom of the press and of academic freedom are to be protected, even against the wrath of disapproval.

"But this very privilege, justifies the expectation that we will have the courage to speak our minds. Since our freedom to speak out lies deep in national tradition, conviction need not bend to hope for gain or favor."

This is the crux. Our freedom—of speech, of press, of research—lying deep in our national tradition, is not under serious legal attack. But our *believability* and, hence our effectiveness, is, unless we have that courage to speak our minds.

Merely rising up to defend our legal rights to free speech and press when it is under attack is not enough. We must take the offensive to clear away these encircling forces of untruth that are the real threat. And we, you in academe and we in journalism, stand in the vanguard of this battle, the major forces dedicated to the search and the propagation of the truth.

The enemies are many. They come in many forms and many disguises. I am certain I do not recognize all of yours in the academic world, nor am I sure I know all ours in the world of news. But some I know, and most of them are mutually antagonistic to us both.

One brigade of the enemy is formed of those who do not understand nor care to tolerate dissent. Since their problem primarily is an intellectual inferiority complex that causes them to shy away from meeting argument and disputation on its own terms, they may be called our present day "know-nothings."

These are the crippled and they come in two groups: The benign who simply prefer not to believe the truth because it does not conform with earlier teachings or superstition, and the wounded bears who, when their beliefs are struck one blow, lash back with an attempt to lacerate all truth and those who would purvey it.

Wounded bears of know-nothingism were those adherents of one prominent candidate in the 1964 elections who seriously railed at the press for reporting what their candidate said rather than what he meant. Does this sound ridiculous to you? It did not to apparently thousands of his followers, and many political reporters and their newspapers and networks have the letters to prove it.

The wounded bears include those hate propagandists who perpetrate an incredible flow of misinformation, lies and calumny on a total of some six-thousand radio programs each week in this country. Their hair-raising stories of the conspiracies against our freedoms and their attacks on all those whose view of patriotism does not coincide exactly with their own, apparently seem credible enough to millions of regular listeners. What a time they must have in sorting out the truth, in determining whom to believe?

Another brigade of enemies of the truth are the "know-somethings." They are those who intellectually understand and accept dissent but who seek to profit by suppression of some part of the truth.

Profit by suppression and by distortion can come in money-bags, as it does in business, in labor and trade organizations, in advertising. Or it can come by accolade and promotion, as it does in government and the military. In either case, intellectual dishonesty is rationalized and rarely is thought given to the eroding effect of such practices on the national morality.

The problem of honesty and truth in the conduct of government is, of course, a matter for which we all bear responsibility in a democracy and which should be a matter of direct concern and immediate action. This is a part of the credibility gap which has brought almost unparalleled cynicism to threaten faith in our democracy at home and in our integrity abroad.

Malcolm Browne, who won a Pulitzer Prize for his reporting from Vietnam over a period of five years, tells of the beginning of our involvement in Vietnam when, during an increasing amount of American military participation, our authorities out there attempted to keep a lid on all information. Our then Ambassador Nolting told Browne that this was an attempt to meet Communist successes that he attributed to the secrecy of their operation, with a secrecy surrounding our own. Obviously, the secrecy did not work and was the beginning of the credibility gap on Vietnam.

Now this misleading of the public has become general armed forces policy and not an accident into which unfortunate individuals have stumbled.

The *New York Times* military correspondent, Hanson Baldwin, noted this quote from a former newspaperman who, as a draftee, taught at the Defense Information School which turns out the Army's Public Information Officers: "The course's main aim is to further goals of the brass, and not the public's right to know. The spirit of public relations prevails while democratic ideals get lip service." And the *Times* quoted another of the school's lecturers, one Captain Gary Werner: "Our task is to prepare the students for their primary obligation, which will be to the people they work for, the executive branch. The public's right to know is not the controlling factor as far as the individual Information Officer is concerned."

Even if there were not a credibility gap, there probably would be an information gap in the Vietnam war, in any case. The mere fact that this is a guerrilla war, fought in small engagements, and not easily measured in the conquest of territory, creates serious problems in reporting. The Army, for instance, resorted to the so-called "body count" as a guide to our success, but this is as subject to error and suspicion as were the claims of the number of aircraft shot down by our bombers in World War II. (Until certain reforms were made in *that* procedure, it appeared that we were destroying the Luftwaffe two or three times over.)

In the present war in the jungles and the swamps, and against an enemy who carries away his dead, if possible, it obviously is not likely that an accurate body count can be achieved. And we have the additional difficulty of confused (to be charitable) accounts from the South Vietnamese given in their own briefings.

The press—and by that generic term I mean all of the reporting media—has not been without its sins in Vietnam. As the military has more than once complained, we have indeed, taken individual squad or platoon actions out of context and blown them up to appear to be the story of an entire battle—an error which can seriously mislead the public as to the nature of victory or defeat. However, I submit that this error has stemmed from the news media's lack of confidence in the over-all briefing on each day's operations, given by the military in Saigon—again a function of honesty.

If the military reports were believed by the press, they would be reported along with the eye-witness correspondents' dispatches from the battlefield. But as it has been—and I should emphasize that this matter has been improved considerably in recent months—the reporter on the scene, even though his field of vision was limited, was a far more trustworthy source than the reports from Information Officers in Saigon who either themselves received inadequate information or were consciously distorting it.

It is this policy of news obscuration which has led the government to deny time after time news stories which later events have forced it to confirm.

U Thant's revelation of Hanoi peace feelers was denied by

Washington, and confirmed only after Eric Sevareid reported them upon Adlai Stevenson's death.

Just this week the Pentagon finally admitted that American air losses in Vietnam were almost double that of previous statements.

A few weeks ago Harrison Salisbury's dispatches in the *New York Times* from Hanoi finally forced admission that we had bombed civilian centers.

Here is the perfect test-tube in which we can examine the culture of the governmental lie. For here were misstatements or, at least, misleading statements which were totally unnecessary.

There is no indication that the American public, having apparently accepted the war, is not prepared to accept the losses it incurs. Or, if the fact is otherwise, then surely the people still have the right to know the truth.

But, perhaps because we who are concerned for the truth have been lax in pointing out with all the fervor necessary the extent of the dissembling, the arrogance of public relations power has fed on itself, and there is reason to believe that much Pentagon secrecy and misstatement is perpetrated thoughtlessly on what it believes to be an unwise and uncaring public. In turn the public has come to accept as fact that it *cannot* believe what comes out of the Pentagon, and the merry-go-round of cynicism spins the faster.

There is another brigade of enemies to the truth who perhaps comprise the most dangerous unit of all. These are the "know-everythings"—the political leaders who intellectually have adopted a belief that the truth can be bent without breaking, that the "little lie," the white lie, is not harmful but might even be helpful in the pursuit of a program to which they are committed. Their slogan, unspoken and perhaps even subconscious, is: "Lying is good for you." This philosophy comes under another name—"news management."

We always have had, and we're always going to have, attempts to manage the news. Everyone—in business, industry, government, university professors—everyone in the world wants the world to think the best of him, wants to put his actions in the best possible light. Sometimes the newspapers go along with this. For instance, wedding announcements, I notice, don't very often go into the bride's earlier intentions, her indecision, her doubts, or her earlier beaux. That's perhaps excusable managed news.

The question here, though, is a little deeper than that. There is a clear and a very present danger to that foundation of our democracy which is the freedom of the press and faith in the honesty of our leaders. It does not come alone from this Administration or its particular attitude toward a favorable image. It is inherent in the age in which we live and a solution to it must be found.

Our problem, of course, is how the nation can be kept informed and how it can be given all the information that is necessary for the viable function of a democracy while denying to the potential enemy the information which is capital to his cause. And even this is not a new problem. But the problem is so compelling in the age of thermo-nuclear weapons and supersonic rockets as to become a new problem.

When a Minuteman can be irrevocably launched from its silo in 15 seconds by the decision of one man, of what value is public debate on the merits of the attack? And when the enemy has the capability of initiating the attack upon the first suspicion that we are contemplating such action, how can we advise the population that such a possibility is even imminent?

Thus, it is not solely that there is neither time nor opportunity for dialogue on the imminent danger and alternative to it, but there is, as well, no time for public reaction, and, more importantly, for discussion.

There is a question as to whether it is even desirable to publicly broadcast the facts. The decision that such broadcast is not desirable then demands the greatest secrecy at the source of the news, the controlled release of all government information and, in the ultimate moment, perhaps even the implantation, as a former spokesman for the Johnson administration has suggested, of the false or the misleading.

Now it's hard to find quarrel with this in the context of the cold war and the ever-present danger. But it is also impossible to quarrel with the fact that it counters the traditional concept of our freedom of the press and the right of the people in a democracy to know. It challenges again the truism that our press has held to be self-evident—that there are no half-way measures in controlling the press. We have laws against libel and against salacious literature and even these are subject to strict judgment and legal redress to protect us against dictatorship by the willful minority. But when we deal with the presentation of factual material, it is impossible to pass laws or edicts that can censor a *Confidential magazine* without touching the *New York Times*.

Who is to determine the national interest if the people themselves cannot? We see all about us in nations deprived of the full exercise of their democratic rights, the extent to which a determination of national interest can go. It reaches the point, almost invariably, where those in power construe *their* continuation in power as in the national interest. That is the ultimate. But each step along the way to that final disaster can be clearly traced. The desire for image, as Madison Avenue has named it, is understandable, but manipulation of the news to achieve it is a dangerous first step.

Another big step is the withholding of news to prevent the people from being "disturbed" because of a sincere belief among the leaders that a predetermined policy is the right and only one, and that public debate of it can only "rock the boat." This is closely related to the "fear of the people" syndrome that has undoubtedly led those with dictatorial bent to clamp the last lock on freedom of the press and public expression. That's an ever-present temptation to every government. We have seen it in its small first manifestations here in the years since World War II as the "restricted" stamp was used in department after department of our government, possibly with even more frequency than that love of the buck-passer, the "for your action" stamp. It was the rampant classification of totally unsensitive material that brought about the Congressional investigations under Representative John Moss that, fortunately, are still going on.

The very facts of our nuclear age, which has brought upon us this new problem of news management, demand that the public know more, not less, about the decisions of government and the men who make them.

In a thermo-nuclear age when more and more frightening power must be vested in fewer and fewer men, and the time allotted for debate and decision is agonizingly restricted, it becomes important that the population be *more* knowledgable, not *less* knowledgable; that it be kept constantly informed of all the details whether they seem at the moment the major ones or the minor ones so that, when the moment of secrecy must be imposed, it can understand the actions of its leaders and not react with violence to misunderstood decisions.

If there is hope of surviving the nuclear holocaust, those who survive must understand through *advance* knowledge why and how the conflict came, else they could turn, in their shock and fury, to an anti-intellectual, anti-government anarchy that would make the Dark Ages look by comparison like the Age of Enlightenment.

I would like to suggest that one of the reasons for the great confusion which wracks this nation today over the Vietnam war is the fact that we were committed without a proper airing of the facts—all the facts.

The Johnson administration and preceeding ones did not level with the American people on the nature or scope of the commitment which, I submit, they themselves must have known was one of the ultimates of our policy.

As one example: In July, 1965, we had some 50,000 troops there. The government told us the number was going to 76,000. And yet out there every military man knew, and frequently said, that 200,000 would be on the ground around the first of the year. By spring of the following year 300,000 was mentioned as an ultimate figure, but already the military was speaking secretly, not for attribution, of 500,000. We have almost reached that figure now.

The Pentagon would have us believe that it has not deliberately misled us, that it would be just as erroneous to reveal possible build-up figures as to underestimate the eventual need. But this is misleading by silence, by failing to take the public into the confidence of those who do the public's business.

At the policy level, *silence* can be as misleading and as deadly a blow to truth and credibility as misstatement.

One of the reasons for America's great confusion as it faced the crisis in Vietnam undoubtedly was the nature of the 1964 Presidental campaign. While President Johnson was re-elected with the greatest majority in our history, that vote in no way constituted a mandate on the Vietnamese war.

President Johnson chose for his own reasons not to debate Barry Goldwater on television or elsewhere. Perhaps because he considered the few comments Mr. Goldwater made on the Vietnam war as irresponsible, he chose not to answer those, and he based little of his own campaign on foreign policy. As a result, the people were denied the opportunity to cast a vote in 1964 on a clear-cut statement of position and policy by either of the candidates, and were even denied a thoughtful elucidation of the problems pertaining to the establishment of a comprehensive policy.

In this regard, the teach-ins and the student demonstrations served an important purpose in bringing home the fact that there was a large body of dissent and that there were some important and intelligent adherents to it. Meanwhile, the slow and tardily-revealed proliferation of the war in Vietnam increased the credibility gap.

There might be a hint to politicians in the experience of this administration on this point. Confrontation in debate during political campaigns—and even by incumbents and their opponents *between* campaigns— might well be a way to restore reality and believability to our political leaders.

The public has become sophisticated. It has read and heard a great deal about Madison Avenue, of ghost writers and political public relations firms, of political campaign organizations which do everything in the creation of a politician's image except select the candidate himself—and I'm not so sure they don't do that.

To put the candidate on his own in a give-and-take debate would bring an elucidation of issues and an opportunity to judge a man on his own knowledge and his own abilities. The lesson would not escape an otherwise jaundiced public.

Perhaps part of the Johnson administration's credibility gap problem stems directly from the fact that it attempts to operate on a consensus when, in fact, it has no mandate on the specifics.

In his book *The Crucible of Leadership,* James M. Burns states: "No matter how benign a government may be, it will be tempted to manipulate public opinion to cover up mistakes and to cast doubt on the patriotism, or at least the honesty of outside critics. The more that government represents a consensus, or claims to, the more tempted it may be to succumb to these tendencies."

As the power of our individual office holders grows with the inevitable growth of government, that which Senator William Fulbright has called arrogance of power, grows too, and not alone in his context of foreign policy, but as well in the treatment of the truth and of those who would speak it.

A newsman of my generation has been able to watch, year by year, the spreading of a tendency among political leaders, to forget what they once knew intellectually, and to react to criticism instead, emotionally. Instead of accepting the newsman and the dissenter as seekers of the truth, they more and more have come to believe that the only responsible newsmen are those clearly committed to their cause.

If there is safety in an informed electorate, there is added security in an informed officialdom. Good newspapers can provide information to government officials that it would take them far too long to get (if indeed they ever got) through secret communications. Why, there may be a bright civil servant not on the distribution lists who has the key that can lock the door on catastrophe or open it to previously undreamed of opportunities for negotiation. This is one of the major strengths of our system. It is this free accession to information, not alone among the population but within the government itself, that the Russian system denies to itself, and it's far the weaker for it.

Government's attempts to manage the news have led to some odd and perhaps fateful decisions—such as that of Secretary of State Dulles in 1957 when he scuttled an agreement with Peking and refused to let American correspondents go into China. Reporting from there even under the limitations imposed by Communist censorship might have helped considerably in this nation's understanding of the nature of the North Vietnamese war against the South and thus possibly have altered history. It might have made considerable difference if we had known then what some of our Far Eastern experts suspect now—that North Vietnam really prefers a policy independent of Red China and might have provided a Titoesque bastion of such independent Communism in Southeast Asia.

Just as there's no such thing as good censorship there is no such thing as a little censorship. And, by the same token, while the "big lie" in the rarest of cases might be justified to save us from imminent disaster, there can be no little lies in the relations of government to the press and, through it, to its people.

We see examples constantly of the wearing away of public confidence in the integrity of government. We could believe, for instance, that the release of government stockpiles of aluminum had no connection with government pressure to hold the line on aluminum prices? Who believed the Department of Defense spokesman who said Marines did not set fire to Cam Ne village when our CBS Newsfilm and newspaper reports clearly illustrated that fact? Who believes those annual cries of despair from the bureaucrats in Washington in the weeks preceding Congress' consideration of the budget? All year those who have told us how well their departments are doing suddenly find themselves in danger of collapse.

Little lies in themselves? White lies? Perhaps. But half-truths or lies, even once indulged in, undermine the government's credibility and feed the fire of scepticism and cynicism that can undermine and destroy our democracy.

When our government is caught in a lie, even if it is admitted after the fact, the damage is not alone to our image in the eyes of the world. Caught but once and we have destroyed endless months or years of good propaganda. A patina of tarnish appears on our symbol of free press that has been the envy of the world.

The reporters who exercise proper scepticism over the news from Washington are rendering a valuable public service and are in the long run helping Washington, not hindering. They are trying to preserve the bulwark of public confidence that would be quickly eroded if many of the releases from the seats of power were printed without question or elaboration.

Because the number one issue on which most of the public attention is focused is the Vietnam war, we should not assume that the credibility gap applies only to it. Recently the *Columbia Jouralism Review* carried a lengthy detailed account of the problems besetting the reporters covering the Office of Economic Opportunity, the war on poverty agency, and they were similar to those encountered by Pentagon reporters.

The OEO information officers denied for instance, reports that VISTA volunteers in Alabama were carrying arms for self-protection. The story later was verified.

"Similarly denied", the *Review* said, "were reports that Rutgers University consultants to the Job Corps Center at Camp Kilmer, New Jersey, were highly dissatisfied with the Center's operations. When the consultants issued a scathing report, OEO explained that its contract with the corporation operating the Center gave the *firm* full control over the release of information.

"Figures released on Job Corps costs per enrollee were revised substantially upwards after they were challenged in Congress."

This article reflects the intimidation with which public officials attempt to challenge newsmen's courage. It reports that John Carmody of the *Washington Post* "has found himself followed by staff members assiduously taking notes" when he visits Job Corps camps.

And the article goes on: "In Washington, reporters who write 'unauthorized' stories about OEO have been questioned about their sources within the Agency—and have discovered that staff members were interrogated by the Inspector General's office to determine whether they were responsible for leaks. OEO officials have challenged the accuracy, integrity—even the sobriety—of reporters who write critical articles. In some instances public denials of stories have been followed by private confirmation—from the same officials who issued the denials."

One of the problems of the publisher and the broadcaster is that public scepticism already has been permitted by a lazy press to taint the press itself. The press appears only to be self-serving when it becomes alarmed over news restrictions, news management, and government lies. The public fails to realize that what is at stake is not a narrow pride of product on the part of the publisher or broadcaster but the citizen's own unquestioned right to know.

Out of the welter of confusion over the Bay of Pigs came President Kennedy's determination to avoid such embarrassment for himself and his government in future crises. He proposed to the newspaper publishers at a convention in April, 1961, shortly after the Bay of Pigs, that there be some system of voluntary censorship to protect vital security matters. He asked for help to try to reconcile the apparently irreconcilable. The two requirements, he said, were "a need for greater public information" and "a need for greater official secrecy". He got a cold shoulder from the publishers, always correctly suspicious of such overtures. It would seem, however, in light of future developments, that the publishers were far less cognizant of the grave problems of news management in an emergency than was the President himself.

Without cooperation from the press in pre-establishing an emergency procedure, President Kennedy found his own solution when the Cuban missile crisis came. He determined that the government action would be secretly coordinated—"orchestrated" was the word we learned then—and that through secrecy and even news management, his administration would speak with one voice.

It must be said that the concept of one voice is rather easily translatable to a frighteningly Orwellian "univoice", a word meaning the crossing of propaganda with genuine information to serve the purposes of the state. Even in its most benign use, one voice is no solution to the problems of democracy in crisis. Perhaps a babble of voices from Washington could prove as confusing to the enemy as it is to our own people, and there may be real diplomatic advantages in such confusion.

I submit that if an administration speaks with one voice and controls every release of that voice's opinion, then perforce every statement from Washington must be considered to be the end result of long study and consultation and bear the imprimatur of the Chief Executive. Under that system there can be no trial balloons and no retreat without loss of face or, in the nuclear age, something more serious.

President Kennedy managed to make his edict of silence stick, but probably only because the crisis was of short duration. Secrecy can be a dangerous game, as his successor discovered in longer crises. Loose talk can be controlled for a short while, but secrets have a way of eventually leaking and attempts to keep them by denying them to the American public through its press are foolhardy at least, fatal at worst.

There must be recognition by the government that American newsmen are not the only "big eared" listeners in Washington. The press of the world and the diplomatic representatives of other nations certainly do not share the national loyalty or the sense of responsibility that well-meaning critics suggest the United States press apply to itself. If the secret is abroad in the drawing rooms of Washington, you can be sure that it's abroad in the parlors of Moscow. The American press would be violating not its patriotism but its sacred trust if it didn't so inform the American public. The Ambassador of Transylvania is entitled to not one more speck of information out of Washington than is any citizen of the United States.

A case for silence might be made in time of delicate diplomatic negotiations with countries that cannot understand the sophisticated demands of full public disclosure in a democracy. It might be necessary for us to hold our tongues and pens temporarily—and only temporarily—but this is only an imperfect solution in an imperfect world. Our goal still should be a candid, truthful bureaucracy where every decision is so clearly dictated by an inherent honesty to our principles that it can be shared with our own people and the rest of the world without fear of misinterpretation or duplicity.

I suggest that in stripping away the veils of secrecy and in exposing to full public gaze the works and decision making processes of government, business, labor, lobbies, trade organizations and the press itself, we can again restore that credibility in one another and in our system of government without which this system cannot long endure.

We, in the community of intellectual leadership—in our press and our universities—have our responsibilities in this crusade—and the exercise of our responsibilities calls for courage. There are big and little ways in which the press must display this courage, and perhaps some or all of them apply to the academician as well.

We need the courage to reject the lurid description or quote that would provide quick profit through sensationalism.

We need the courage to reject the frequently unnecessary pressure of deadline. The reporter must, of course, record first impressions. They are living, current history, free of the distortion of second thoughts and frequent re-telling. But the use of such material frequently requires and does not get the best, considered, editorial judgment free of deadline pressures.

We need the courage to criticize even when it hurts the innocent. For instance, we cannot, although some do, withhold criticism of Washington policy when somehow it seems to be letting down the soldiers on the line.

We need the courage to reject the favor of the newsmakers. Newsmen must not become part of the establishment, and this is an invitation that even the strongest among us find hard to refuse. We must preserve access to the inner circle without becoming members of it.

We need the courage to reject a sort of conformity of camaraderie among our colleagues. If we believe we perceive the truth while others around us seem blind to it, we need the courage of our convictions.

We need courage to reject the warmth of our neighbors and to face social ostracism in our pursuit of the truth.

We of the press must remind ourselves that we can discharge our responsibility to the truth best by reportorial practice rather than editorial alarm.

We must be better newsmen, sharpening our diligence against fraud and deceit and fearlessly exposing those who practice it. We must be sceptical, so that the people won't become cynical.

And most of all, you of the universities and we of the press, need the courage and the stamina to *teach* the truth and a love of it so that the day will come again when the majority of this nation respect it.

We need to teach the need for personal, eternal, life-long vigilance in the search for truth.

If we do our jobs well, the day will come, sooner than the most optimistic might dare predict, when the demand for truth and honesty in all human relations will overcome the lethargy and cynicism which today threatens us.

The Persians are at the gates. Arise Spartans!

9

THE BELIEVABILITY OF BROADCASTING

When Vice President Agnew, in November 1969, unleashed his attack upon the news media, he was following, albeit with unique linguistic and philosophic departures, a long line of predecessors. Somewhere in the history of our Republic there may have been a high government official who said he had been treated fairly by the press, but for the life of me, however, I can't think of one.

Mr. Agnew's attacks, of course, were particularly alarming because of their sustained virulence and intimidating nature. But the Vice President was simply joining the chorus (or, seeing political opportunity, attempting to lead it) of those who have appointed themselves critics of the television medium. Well, I don't like everything I see on television either, but I am frank to say I'm somewhat sick and mighty tired of broadcast journalism being constantly dragged into the operating room and dissected, probed, swabbed, and needled to see what makes it tick.

I'm tired of sociologists, psychologists, pathologists, educators, parents, bureaucrats, politicians, and other special interest groups presuming to tell us what is news or where our responsibilities lie.

Or perhaps I'm phrasing this wrong. It is not those who squeeze us between their slides and hold us under their

Address at the Sigma Delta Chi convention, November 12, 1970.

microscopes with whom my patience has grown short. The society *should* understand the impact of television upon it. There are aspects of it that need study so that the people can cope with an entirely revolutionary means of communication. Those who disagree with our news coverage have every right to criticize. We can hardly claim rights to free press and free speech while begrudging those rights to our critics. Indeed, that would seem to be what some of them would like to do to us. So believing, it clearly cannot be the responsible critics or serious students of the TV phenomenon with whom I quarrel. I am provoked more by those in our craft who, like wide-eyed country yokels before the pitchman, are losing sight of the pea under the shell.

We must expose the demagogues who would undermine this nation's free media for personal or partisan political gain. That is news. And we should not withhold our cooperation from serious studies of the medium. But we must not permit these matters to divert us from our task, or confuse us as to what that task is.

I don't think it is any of our business what the moral, political, social, or economic effect of our reporting is. I say let's get on with the job of reporting the news—and let the chips fall where they may. I suggest we concentrate on doing our job of telling it like it is and not be diverted from that exalted task by the apoplectic apostles of alliteration.

Now, a fair portion of what we do is not done well. There are things we are not doing that we ought to do. There are challenges that we have not yet fully met. We are a long way from perfection. Our problems are immense, and they are new and unique.

A major problem is imposed by the clock. In an entire

half-hour news broadcast we speak only as many words as there are on two-thirds of one page of a standard newspaper. Clearly, the stricture demands tightness of writing and editing, and selection, unknown in any other form of journalism. But look what we do with that time. There are twenty items in an average newscast—some but a paragraph long, true, but all with the essential information to provide at least a guide to our world that day. Film clips that, in a way available to no other daily medium, introduce our viewers to the people and the places that make the news; investigative reports (pocket documentaries) that expose weakness in our democratic fabric (not enough of these, but we're coming along), feature film reports that explore the byways of America and assure us that the whole world hasn't turned topsy-turvy; graphics that in a few seconds communicate a great deal of information; clearly identified analysis, or commentary, on the news—I think that is quite a package.

The transient, evanescent quality of our medium—the appearance and disappearance of our words and picture at almost the same instant—imposes another of our severe problems. Most of us would agree that television's greatest asset is the ability to take the public to the scene—the launch of a spaceship, a Congressional hearing, a political convention, or a disaster (in some cases these are not mutually exclusive). Live coverage of such continuing, developing events presents the radio-television newsman with a challenge unlike any faced by the print reporter. The newspaper legman, rewrite man, and editor meet the pressure of deadlines and must make hard decisions fast and accurately. But multiply their problems and decisions a thousandfold and you scarcely have touched on the problems of the electronic journalist broadcasting live. Even with the most intensive coverage it still is difficult and frequently impossible to get all the facts and get all of them straight as a complex and occasionally violent story is breaking all around. We do have to fill in additional material on subsequent broadcasts, and there is the danger that not all the original audience is there for the fuller explanation.

When a television reporter, in the midst of the riot or the floor demonstration or the disaster, dictates his story, he is not talking to a rewrite man but directly to the audience. There is no editor standing between him and the reader. He will make mistakes, but his quotient for accuracy must be high or he is not long for this world of electronic journalism. We demand a lot of these on-the-scene television reporters. I for one think they are delivering in magnificent fashion.

Directors of an actuality broadcast, like newspaper photo editors, have several pictures displayed on the monitors before them. But they, unlike their print counterparts, do not have ten minutes, or five, or even one minute to select the picture their audience will see. Their decision is made in seconds. Theirs is a totally new craft in journalism, but they have imbued it with all the professionalism and sense of responsibility and integrity of the men of print. Of course we make mistakes, but how few are the errors compared to the fielding chances!

Our profession is encumbered, even as it is liberated, by the tools of our trade. It is a miracle—this transmission of pictures and voices through the air, the ability to take the whole world to the scene of a single event. But our tools still are somewhat gross. Miniaturization and other developments eventually will solve our problem, but for the moment our cameras and our lights and our tape trucks and even our microphones are obtrusive. It is probably true that their presence can alter an event, and it probably also is true that they alter it even more that the presence of reporters with pad and pencil, although we try to minimize our visibility. But I think we should not be too hasty in adjudging this as always a bad thing. Is it not salutary that the government servant, the politician, the rioter, the miscreant knows that he is operating in the full glare of publicity, that the whole world is watching?

Consider political conventions. They have been a shambles of democratic malfunction since their inception, and printed reports through the years haven't had much effect in reforming them. But now that the voters have been taken to them by television, have sat through the sessions with the delegates and seen the political establishment operate to suppress rather than develop the democratic dialogue, there is a stronger reform movement than ever before, and the chances of success seem brighter.

I would suggest that the same is true of the race rioters and the student demonstrators, whatever the justice of the point they are trying to make. Of course they use television. Hasn't that always been the point of the demonstrator—to attract attention to his cause? But the *excesses* of the militants on ghetto streets and the nation's campuses, shown by television with almost boring repetition, tend to repel rather than enlist support, and this is a lesson I hope and *believe* that rational leaders are learning.

Scarcely anyone would doubt that television news has expanded to an immeasurable degree the knowledge of many people who either cannot or do not read. We have broadened the interests of another sizable group whose newspaper reading is confined to the headlines, sports, and comics. We are going into homes of the untutored, teaching underprivileged and disadvantaged who have never known a book. We are exposing them to a world they scarcely knew existed, and while advertisements and entertainment programming whet their thirst for a way of life they believe beyond them, we show them that there are people and movements, inside and outside the Establishment, that are trying to put the good things within their reach.

Without any intent to foster revolution, by simply doing our job as journalists with ordinary diligence and an extraordinary new medium, we have awakened a sleeping giant. No wonder we have simultaneously aroused the ire of those who are comfortable with the status quo. Many viewers happily settled in their easy chairs under picture windows that frame leafy boughs and flowering bushes and green grass resent our parading the black and bearded, the hungry and unwashed through their living rooms, reminding them that there is another side of America that demands their attention. It is human nature to avoid confronting the unpleasant. No one *wants* to hear that "our boys" are capable of war crimes, that our elected officials are capable of deceit or worse. I think I can safely say that there are few of us who want to report such things. But as professional journalists we have no more discretion in whether to report or not to report when confronted with the facts than does a doctor in deciding to remove a gangrenous limb.

If it *happened*, the people are entitled to know. There is no condition that can be imposed on that dictum without placing a barrier (censorship) between the people and the truth—at once as fallible and corrupt as only self-serving men can make it. The barrier can be built by government—overtly by dictatorship or covertly with propaganda on the political stump, harassment by subpoena, or abuse of the licensing power. Or the barrier can be built by the news media themselves. If we permit our news judgment to be colored by godlike decisions as to what is good for our readers, listeners, or viewers, we are building a barrier—no matter how pure our motives. If we permit friendship with sources to slow our natural reflexes, we also build a barrier. If we lack courage to face the criticism and consequences of our reporting, we build barriers.

But of all the barriers that we might put between the people and the truth, the most ill-considered is the one that some would erect to protect their profits. In all media, under our precious free enterprise system, there are those who believe performance can only be measured by circulation or ratings. The newspaper business had its believers long before we were on the scene. They practiced editing by readership survey. Weak-willed but greedy publishers found out what their readers *wanted* to read and gave it to them—a clear abdication of their duties as journalists and, I would submit, a nail in the coffin of newspaper believability.

Today, before the drumfire assault of the hysterical Establishment and the painful complaints of a frightened populace, there are many in our business who believe we should tailor our news reports to console our critics. They would have us report more good news and play down the war, revolution, social disturbance. There certainly is nothing wrong with good news. In fact, by some people's lights we report quite a lot of it: an anti-pollution bill through Congress, a report that the cost of living isn't going up as fast as it was last month, settlement of a labor dispute, the announcement of a medical breakthrough, plans for a new downtown building. There isn't anything wrong either with the stories that tell us what is right about America, that reminds us that the virtues that made this nation strong still exist and prosper despite the turmoil of change.

But when "give us the good news" becomes a euphemism for "don't give us so much of that bad news"—and in our business one frequently means the other—the danger signal must be hoisted.

It is possible that some news editors have enough time allotted by their managements to cover all the significant news of their areas—much of it, presumably, in the "bad" category—and still have time left over for a "good news" item or two. But for many and certainly those at the network level, that is not the case. To crowd in the "happy" stories would mean crowding out material of significance. Some good-news advocates know this, and it is precisely what they want: to suppress the story of our changing society in the hope that if one ignores evil it will go away.

Others simply are tired of the constant strife. They would like a little relief from the daily budget of trouble that reminds them of the hard decisions they as citizens must face. But can't they see that pandering to the innocent seeking relief is to yield to those who would twist public opinion to control our destiny?

It is no coincidence that these manipulative methods parallel those adopted half a century ago by Russian revolutionaries also seeking the surest means to bend the population to their will. You will not find bad news in Russian newspapers or on broadcast media. There are no reports of riots, disturbances of public order, muggings or murders, train, plane, or auto wrecks. There are no manifestations of race prejudice, disciplinary problems in army ranks. There is no exposure of malfeasance in public office—other than that which the government chooses to exploit for its own political purposes. There is no dissent over national policy, no argument about the latest weapons system.

There is a lot of good news—factories making their quotas, happy life on the collective farm, successes of Soviet diplomacy, difficulties in the United States. The system works. Without free media—acerbic, muckraking, irreverent—the Soviet people are placid drones and the Soviet Establishment runs the country the way it wants it run.

Since it is hard to know the real motives in others' minds—indeed, it is hard sometimes to know our own motives—and since few are likely to admit that they would seek to suppress dissent from Establishment norms, it would be wrong to ascribe such Machiavellian connivance to the good-news advocates. The only trouble is that the other, more likely motive—profiting from the news by pandering to public taste—is almost as frightening. To seek the public's favor by presenting the news it wants to hear is to fail to understand the function of the media in a democracy. We are not in the business of winning popularity contests, and we are not in the entertainment business. It is not our job to please anyone except Diogenes.

The newsman's purpose is contrary to the goal of almost everyone who shares the airwaves with us, and perhaps we should not be too harsh with those executives with the ultimate responsibility for station and network management. We are asking a great deal of them. For seventeen of the eighteen hours during an average broadcast day their job is to win friends and audience. They and we live on how successfully they do this difficult job.

But then we ask them to turn a deaf ear to the complaints of those dissatisfied with what we present in the remaining minutes of the day. We ask them to be professionally schizoid—and that would seem to be a lot to ask. But is it, really? After all, in another sense, as journalists we live this life of dual personality. There is not a man who can truthfully say that he does not harbor in his breast prejudice, bias, strong sentiments pro and con on some if not all the issues of the day.

Yet it is the distinguishing mark of the professional journalist that he can set aside these personal opinions in reporting the day's news. None of us succeeds in this task in all instances, but we know the assignment and the pitfalls, and we succeed far more often than we fail or than our critics would acknowledge. We have a missionary duty to try to teach this basic precept of our craft to those of our bosses who have not yet learned it. We in broadcasting, at least, cannot survive as a major news medium if we fail.

We were well on the way before the current wave of politically inspired criticism. In my twenty years in broadcasting I have seen more and more station owners taking courage from their news editors, tasting the heady fruit of respect that can be won by the fearless conveyor of the truth. Some years ago William Allen White wrote that "nothing fails so miserably as a cowardly newspaper." I suspect he spoke not only of commercial failure but of the greater failure: not winning the confidence of the people. A radio or television station also can fail this test of courage, and when it does its owner wins not a community's respect and gratitude but its contempt.

Broadcast management is going to need a stiff backbone in the days ahead—not only for its own well-being but for the good of us all. We are teetering on the brink of a communications crisis that could undermine the foundation of our democracy that is a free and responsible press. We all know the present economic background. We in radio and television with our greater impact and our numerous outlets have forced many of our print competitors out of business. It is a rare American city today that has more than one newspaper. And yet I think most of us will acknowledge that we are not an adequate substitute for the newspapers whose demise we have hastened. We cannot supply the wealth of detail the informed citizen needs to judge the performance of his city, county, or state. If we do our jobs thoroughly, however, we can be a superb monitor over the monopoly newspaper, assuring that it does not by plot, caprice, or inadvertence miss a major story.

We *can* be, that is, if we are left alone to perform that essential journalistic function. The trouble is that broadcast media are not free; they are government licensed. The power to make us conform is too great to lie forever dormant. The ax lies there temptingly for use by any enraged administration, Republican, Democrat, or Wallaceite. We are at the mercy of the whim of politicians and bureaucrats, and whether they choose to chop us down or not, the mere existence of their power is an intimidating and constraining threat.

So on one side there is a monopoly press that may or may

not choose to present views other than those of the domineerin majority, on the other side a vigorously competitive but federally regulated broadcast industry, most of whose time is spent currying popular—that is, majority—favor. This scarcely could be called a healthy situation. There is a real danger that the free flow of ideas, the vitality of minority views, even the dissent of recognized authorities could be stifled in such an atmosphere.

We newsmen, dedicated as we are to freedom of press and speech and the presentation of all viewpoints no matter how unpopular, must work together, regardless of our medium, to clear the air while there is still time. We must resist every new attempt at government control, intimidation, or harassment. And we must fight tenaciously to win through Congress and the courts guarantees that will free us forever from the present restrictions. We must stand together and bring the power of our professional organizations to bear against those publishers and broadcast managers who fail to understand the function of a free press. We must keep our own escutcheons so clean that no one who would challenge our integrity could hope to succeed.

If we do these things, we can preserve, and re-establish where it has faded, the confidence of the people whose freedom is so indivisibly linked with ours.